D1429194

THE WORLD
of Football!!!
ACCORDING
TO ATHLETICO
MINCE

THE WORLD
of Football ↑
ACCORDING
TO ATHLETICO
MINCE*

The Book of Bob
& Andy's Hit Podcast

*8% FOOTBALL CONTENT GUARANTEED!

JOHN BLAKE

Published by John Blake Publishing Ltd
3 Bramber Court, 2 Bramber Road,
London W14 9PB, England

www.johnblakebooks.com

www.facebook.com/johnblakebooks 🇫
twitter.com/jblakebooks 🇹

First published in hardback in 2017

ISBN: 978 1 78606 250 5

British Library Cataloguing-in-Publication Data:

A catalogue record for this book is available from the British Library.

Design by www.envydesign.co.uk

Printed in Great Britain by CPI Group (UK) Ltd

1 3 5 7 9 10 8 6 4 2

Papers used by John Blake Publishing are natural, recyclable
products made from wood grown in sustainable forests. The manufacturing
processes conform to the environmental
regulations of the country of origin.

Every attempt has been made to contact the relevant
copyright-holders, but some were unobtainable. We would be
grateful if the appropriate people could contact us.

John Blake Publishing is an imprint of Bonnier Publishing
www.bonnierpublishing.com

Special thanks to Mark Robson and Jim Campbell

CONTENTS

CONTENTS

INTRODUCTION

ANDY SAYS... 'Back in early 2016, I found myself at the Royal London Men's Tit and Heart Hospital, after a concerned blood relative had gifted me a voucher for a full tit MOT. In case you're wondering, I underwent a vigorous five-hour set of tests and checks and came up trumps in every category – curvature, buoyancy, firmness, density and protrusion.

'As I headed towards the exit, with my head and my breasts held high, I spotted a broken figure of a man slouched in the corner of a day room, waiting to be discharged. His eyes met mine and he held up a sign that simply read "Help". I approached him and he whispered his story to me as best he could.

'This battered husk of a man had recently undergone a triple heart bypass operation and his life had been hanging in the balance. He claimed that no one had been to visit him in days, and that his wife had chosen to take an extended holiday in the Maldives while he was recuperating.

'I took pity on him, helping him to get home and, once there, I fed him some sugared water from a spoon, which he seemed to respond to. I returned to visit him every day after that, helping him to restore his strength by giving him special smoothies that I had concocted – one was made from blended buttered Weetabix, another from air-fried chicken dippers and another from a medley of flavours from the Fridge Raiders range of snacks. All of them were blended with a creamy white Dolmio lasagne sauce.

'His recovery was startling and, during one visit, he was visibly excited as he was due to be visited by an important council dignitary from his home town. He was hoping that the visit might include some kissing and he asked me if I would apply some lipstick for him in advance – together we picked out a deep shade of red and he soon looked like a sweet, sweet fancy boy.

'We both had a shared interest in football, and we began having long, hilarious conversations about various aspects of 'the beautiful game'. It occurred to me that these informal chats would make for entertaining podcasts – he agreed, so we booked a studio and looked forward to releasing our podcasts to the nation.

'On the day of the first recording, his heart seized up and he died – the coroner later said he'd never seen such a build-up of trans fats in the system of someone who had only just undergone triple bypass surgery.

'Undeterred, I rang up Bob Mortimer and he agreed to do

the podcast instead, and Athletico Mince was born. This is the book of it.'

BOB SAYS... 'How very fucking hell!'

A HISTORY
OF FOOTBALL

PART ONE
THE BEGINNING YEARS

January 1862: Football as we know it is invented after MPs decide that the lower orders need something for them to enthuse and argue about, in order to distract them from their horrific living and working conditions. The first team to be founded is Notts County but, as no other teams are founded until 1863, County have no one to play against for over a year. The players spend most of their time training and visiting other towns to see if anyone else has formed a football team yet.

December 1878: Goalposts are used for the first time since the game was invented. The team of toffs at Harrow boarding school pay four local working-class boys a farthing between them to mark out the goals, with each boy stripped naked, painted white and ordered to hold a piece of string at head height. When one of the 'posts' faints in the sub-zero temperatures, the home-team captain carries the lad from the pitch and brings him round with a nip of brandy. He and the young lad are later married in a secret ceremony in Blackheath.

June 1914: Dogs.

May 1921: Everton defender Harold Haroldson vanishes after a tragic training-ground accident. A golden eagle swoops down and picks Haroldson up by the scruff of the neck before flying off with him. The player is never seen again, although some believe he is the anonymous, mythical bird-man who emerges from a Shropshire wood in 1927, covered in feathers and whooping like a fog horn.

3

May 1931: Arsenal and Preston North End play out a thrilling 23-23 draw in the first ever extra-time final at Wembley, following a dull, goalless ninety minutes. The players are completely exhausted for the added thirty minutes and strong, strange winds take any above-average pass swirling towards the back of the net.

Only six players are able to play in the replay the following day, which is abandoned at 1-0 when a golden eagle swoops down and gathers up the ball, dropping it in Arsenal's net. The fact that it is the tenth anniversary of the Harold Haroldson incident adds a chilling extra dimension to it all.

November 1946: Derby County's Billy Wincup has his head temporarily removed when manager Stan Abbott allows the players to play a five-a-side training game with samurai swords that his brother-in-law brought back from the war. Luckily, Wincup's head is put in a bucket of ice and is quickly reattached, albeit initially the wrong way round.

December 1948: Nottingham Forest defender Charles Diablo stuns football and the nation by revealing that his life and career is guided by Satan. Diablo says, 'Lucifer is my prince and, each time my studs dig into the turf, I reach out to him and he grooms me. If we can get past West Brom in the quarter-finals and get a favourable draw in the last four, the FA Cup Final will be my Perdition. Follow me.' God-fearing West Brom wing-half Stanley Belpitt says, 'Give me five minutes with Charles. Just five minutes. I will heal him with my love.'

January 1952: With London in the grip of the Great Smog, matches in the capital are played as normal but decided by a unique method. Unable to see more than a few feet in front of them, each team has to declare how many goals they believe they scored and conceded at the end of ninety minutes. Then, after calculating the result by using a special equation supplied by the Department of Mathematics, the referee announces the score to the crowd by blowing the number of goals on two differently pitched bugles.

May 1953: The FA allow the use of iron shin pads, claiming that injuries from mistimed tackles will be a thing of the past. The shin pads are abandoned after just two weeks following a series of smashed-foot injuries and two fatigue-related deaths from players running around for ninety minutes with lumps of iron strapped to their shins.

May 1955: Wally Hart scores what is still regarded as the best ever goal in an FA Cup Final, for Tottenham against Wolves. Picking the ball up in his own half, he drills it into the pitch with such force that it tunnels its way under the Wolves midfield before surfacing on the edge of their area. Hart continues his run and collects the ball as it comes out of the ground, smashing it past the keeper, winning the Cup and getting a kiss off a lass into the bargain.

June 1956: The very first European Cup Final is played, between Real Madrid and Stade de Reims. The Spanish side win 4-3, but the final is very different to the kind we see today. As an experiment, the match is played in complete darkness, kicking off at 3am. Also, each player has a ball to himself, but most of them are soon burst by snipers who crouch in the corners of the stands. After the match, the losing French side must line up as the winners collect the trophy and stand motionless, allowing the Madrid players to ruffle their hair and pinch their cheeks in a patronising style. Then they are executed by the excited snipers.

October 1956: The FA clamps down on the new wave of rock-'n'-roll-based goal celebrations following complaints by six different religious leaders. Most guilty are Manchester United's infamous Busby Babes, whose intricate jiving routines during their 7-1 win over Sheffield Wednesday see the evening kick-off finally end at 2.15am the following morning.

May 1957: It's a sad day for Luton Town fans as the last kennel is removed from the terracing of their Kenilworth Road home. The ground had been world famous for its rows and rows of kennels, which supporters would crouch in to watch the match, but the board decides that they have to go. Chairman Bill Douglas says, 'There's nothing I enjoy more than seeing the heads of our fans poking out of their kennels on a Saturday afternoon, barking the boys on to victory, but they're taking up too much space. We've got a capacity of nine hundred and seventy-three and we could have twenty times as many in if they all stood up like normal humans.' Ironically, most of the die-hard fans stopped coming once the kennels were removed, as they were unable to adapt to spending an entire ninety minutes without trying to lie down and lick their own testicles.

May 1960: Walter Russell, the chairman of Scottish strugglers East Fife, sells the club for £170 to a passing rag-and-bone man. Tired of mounting debts and poor performances, Russell offloads the ground and entire staff to Willie Muir, who takes it all away by horse and cart over the following days. A consortium is formed to take over the ownership of the club, but they are forced to buy a brand-new stadium, picking up a non-league one for £400 from a nearby scrap yard.

July 1961: A pre-season friendly between Merthyr Tydfil and West Bromwich Albion is abandoned after four of the Welsh side's players' tunnel their way to freedom midway through the first half. It emerges that they had been kept captive by the club as they hadn't paid their 'dinner money', a popular non-league form of illegal player taxation. The players use cutlery to dig their way out of the ground and take refuge in a local zoo, where they stay for the next eighteen months until the case comes to court.

November 1962: Arsenal's stars are spearheading the fashion for fitness in football by banning their players from smoking during games. Prior to the ban, most of their back four and midfield could be seen lighting up at least once during a half, as could most other players in the First Division. The ban sees an increase in tetchiness among Arsenal's players, leading to fifteen more red cards and a battle against relegation.

May 1965: Forfar Athletic drop their controversial seventy-five-year-old nickname, 'The Greedy Bastards'. The moniker hails from the early days of the club, when players had to weigh in excess of eighteen stone before they could play. Any player who turned up for a match short of this minimum weight was force-fed steak and kidney pies in the dressing room until he made the weight – a practice known as 'forfaring'. The club announces that its new nickname is to be 'The Knicker-Sniffers'.

July 1966: England win the World Cup.

September 1966: Middlesbrough have a request to postpone their match with Bristol Rovers turned down by the FA, after their excuse of 'We've got a dirty pitch' isn't deemed worthy of postponement.

May 1967: Ron Ronson manages both FA Cup finalists after being poached by the opposition during the first half of the match. Ronson is the West Bromwich Albion boss as the final kicks off, but is passed a note from Aston Villa chairman Dick Hastings after the Baggies take an early 2-0 lead offering him a 'double your money' deal. He promptly quits as West Brom manager while the match is being played and appears on the Villa bench for the start of the second half, guiding his new team to a dramatic 3-2 win and Wembley glory.

August 1967: Fans of Notts County are in for a pleasant surprise when they attend the club's away fixtures. That's because their transport is being laid on free of charge by the club, in the form of an 80ft-long Chinese dragon that chairman Vic Nancy picked during a business trip to the Far East. However, the dragon is not motorised and fans find they have to adopt the traditional 'Flintstones' method in order to power it and reach their destination.

December 1967: Leicester City boss Ron Tynan becomes the first football manager to use a swear word on national TV, leading to a lifetime ban for him from both the BBC and ITV. Following a 4-0 defeat at Aston Villa, Tynan tells an interviewer, 'Those c***s were a f***ing disgrace out there today. I've never seen a bigger bunch of s**t-for-brains, c**ksucking motherf***ers together on one field at the same f***ing time in my entire life.'

As the interviewer removes his own flat cap and tries to stuff it in the manager's mouth, Tynan adds, 'They're not fit to sniff the f***ing skidmarks in my f***ing granny's f***ing undercrackers. F***ing s***heads, the lot of them,' before downing half a bottle of scotch and running out of the ground waving a gun.

April 1968: Everton boss Harry Catterick reveals the secret behind the team's FA Cup run – he and the players refuse to find out their opposition until they take to the field. Catterick says, 'We did it in the third round and it worked so we've stuck with it. It's become a kind of superstition.' The players all get on the team coach wearing blindfolds and don't remove them until they're in the tunnel, just minutes before the kick-off. The Toffees' manager adds, 'If we get to the final, we plan to get a hypnotist in so that the lads have got no idea what any of it means.'

October 1968: The last of the Pirate Leagues finally runs aground. The leagues were formed by hundreds of teams who had been forbidden to join the official Football League, playing their matches instead on board cramped ships in the North Sea and posting the results back to anxious shore-bound fans via a message in a bottle. The practice finally dies out when all of those involved realise it is a complete waste of time.

January 1969: Non-league Tiverton Town set a record of 102 consecutive league defeats following a 19-2 loss away at Salisbury. Manager Jack Walton refuses to blame the abysmal run on the fact that nine of his regular starting eleven are under the age of four.

February 1969: Manchester United fear that superstar George Best may be out for six months, as his injury nightmare continues. The club doctor says, 'We thought we could replace his troublesome hamstrings with new ones made from elongated bubble gum, but it has not worked the same way that it worked on the club mice. We need to think again, it seems.'

October 1969: German striker and notorious hippy Erik Klanger turns down a lucrative move to SV Hamburg after the club refuse to pay his wages in flower petals. Klanger insists that he has no need for cash and would prefer petals instead, which he will distribute among the poorest areas of the city every afternoon after training. Klanger quits the game three months later and, within four years, he is the vice president of SchnauserCorp, Germany's largest debt-collecting and gorilla-exporting company.

A BEGINNER'S GUIDE TO OBSERVATIONAL COMEDY

Hello. I am the Secret Stand-Up Comedian. I am definitely a real comedian, who has enjoyed major successes at every level in the comedy game, from sweaty clubs to massive, soulless, cash-generating arenas. I know everything there is to know about cracking jokes and have been asked to analyse the observational-comedy stylings of Bob and Andy from Athletico Mince.

I have reproduced some of their finest routines for you, and added my own expert comments. I am not Jack Whitehall.

BOB'S COMEDY

'Listen, right, don't you hate it when a mental bloke gets on the train and all the other seats are empty but he sits next to you, so you have to put your brass hand case on your lap?'

You're not allowed to say 'mental' any more.

'Have you ever noticed on the train that the toilet lock never works so you have to jam the mechanism with your brass hand? Have you noticed that?'

Not something that happens often. Also, the brass-hand thing is logistically vague and would confuse audiences.

'Don't you hate it... have you ever noticed on the train,

the conductor's hands are always, like, covered in fabric conditioner or Swarfega and it makes your brass hand all tacky when he gives you your ticket back? Have you noticed that?'

This is nonsense. Perhaps Bob dreamed this scenario.

'You go to the station and it says your train's cancelled, so you ask the fella why it's cancelled and he says, "I don't know." So you ask him when's the next train and he says, "I don't know." So you ask him if you can get a refund and he says, "I don't know." So you ask if you can buy some brass-hand oil on the concourse and he says, "I don't know." Have you noticed that?'

Brass-hand oil is available on almost every major station concourse in Britain. As a brass-hand user, Bob should know that, and this oversight causes the gag to fall horribly flat.

'Eehhh, listen, eehhhh, are you like me? Whenever I fill out an application, in the part that says "In an emergency, who should we notify", I always put "DOCTOR". I mean, what's me mother going to do – she's got a brass hand!'

What if the emergency is a fire? Another deeply flawed premise.

'Have you ever noticed, ehhh... have you ever noticed that children can be a bit unruly? For example, at a party, sports event or family picnic? Have you ever noticed that?'

Weak. Should never have got past the draft stage.

'Ehhhhh. Ehhhhh. Ehhhh. Ehhhhhhhhhhhhhhh. I saw six men kicking and punching the mother-in-law. Me neighbour said, "Are you going to help or what?" I said, "No, six should be enough – one of them has a brass hand and he's fucking lethal!"'

This is an old Les Dawson gag that Bob has tarted up with another tedious mention of his brass hand. Also, violence against women is not allowed in comedy any more.

'Ehhhh... why is it called Alcoholics Anonymous? The first thing you do is say, "My name is Robert and I have a brass hand." Ehhhhh?'

Ridiculous.

'Ehhhh... if you think no one cares whether you're alive, try missing a couple of payments on your brass-hand hire!'

This is 2017 – statistics show that 99.4 per cent of brass-hand users now own their brass hands, with hiring very much a thing of the past. Like most of Bob's material, this is a stale throwback.

'Ehhhhh, ehhh, ehhhhhhhhhh, have you ever noticed when you're in a hotel, like, and the lead on the kettle is so short that you have to put the kettle on the floor next to the socket – which is really difficult with my brass hand.'

Like most travelling comedians, Bob is deluded into thinking that everyone spends most of their time cooped up in cheap hotels. A fatal comedic error.

'Listen, ehhh, have you noticed, every time you go in the toilet in your hotel room, you just hear AEEEERRRRR from the air con and then it goes off after about twenty minutes, then you go for a wee and it goes back on again and you go, "Awwww, God, I forgot about that!" and your brass hand starts to vibrate?'

This seems to be a gag about a fault that might very well be specific only to Bob's brass hand. His best course of action would probably to get it serviced at an authorised dealership.

'Eeehhhh, what's it like, right... what's it like when you're staying in a hotel and you go in the shower and someone's set it at about two thousand degrees, and it all gets in your brass-hand mechanism? And then you can't work out how to use the stupid plug 'cos all the plugs are stupid. You know, the plug in the sink – and you have to unscrew your brass hand and use that. How do you use that? What are you meant to press? So you have to put your brass hand in the hole. And the window's hardly open – have you ever noticed? How am I meant to get my brass hand through there and shoo the pigeons, you know what I mean?'

This is just deranged. Assuming that the entire audience hadn't just got up and left by this point, Bob would be very lucky not to be booed off for this clumsy, desperate routine.

'Ehh, ehh, ehh, have you ever noticed, as soon as there's an inch of fucking snow, everyone and their monkey is out and about at the local hillock with a sledge. Yeah? Have you noticed that? And there's always one perfect family that has the Rolls-Royce of sledges and all you have is a Papa John's pizza box to use, ehh? Ehh? And after a couple of goes, the ink runs from the box design and stains your brass hand! Have you noticed that?'

Possible paid-for product placement here, either by Rolls-Royce or Papa John's. More likely to be the latter. Still, very unedifying.

'Ehh. Ehh. Ehh, ehh, ehh, ehh, ehhhhhhhhhh... have you ever noticed, all of us fellas, we've got a drawer at home that's got all your bits of shit in? You know, watch batteries, hinges, old charger cables and that – but, but you can never find your brass-hand oil in there, can you?'

Another woeful piece of material. Most brass-hand users keep their oil on a shelf in order to avoid spillages.

'Ehh. Ehh. Ehh, ehh, ehh, ehh... do you remember old-fashioned trousers? You know, with button flies and the buttons for your braces? What a lovely, funny memory, eh, boys and girls? But... you could never fix your braces with your brass hand, could you? Unless you're fucking Dynamo – you know, the magic Yorkshireman.'

Bob proves here that he isn't fit to lace the boots of Dynamo.

ANDY'S COMEDY

'Ehhhh, ehhhhh, listen though, I tell you who you don't see much of these days... the IRA.'

Short, sweet and factually accurate. Here's hoping we don't see the IRA ever again.

'The landline rang the other day. I didn't answer it. Could have been anyone. Could have been the IRA!'

Nice. Great use of nostalgia along with a call-back to the previous IRA gag.

'Right. Ehhhhh. Right... listen! Have you been watching the Olympics? Have you seen it? Did you see the marathon? How come they don't call it the Snickers? Ehhhhhh?'

Now THIS is how to do product placement. A lovely dollop of nostalgia too – hope Snickers showed their appreciation and sent Andy a year's supply! If not, it's not too late, and they could send it c/o the publisher of this book.

'Here... listen. Do you remember the proper Batman? The proper one from the nineteeeeeen sixtieeeeeeees – when he used to be in a good mood? Not the new one, when he's always got a cob on about summat.'

Nostalgia again but with a modern-day reference. A perfect gag for keeping the olds and the youngs engaged.

'Ehhhh, ehhhhh, listen. Listen to this one. What's the deal with Shetland ponies? What's that all about? They're just like proper horses but you can fit them into the back of a Transit van. What do you want to put a horse in a van for? Who's fucking stupid idea was that? Ehhhhhh? Ehhhhh? What? Ehhhhhhh?'

This is a masterclass of visualisation. If you're not currently thinking of a Shetland pony in the back of a van and rocking with mirth, you simply have no funny bone.

'Alright, listen, here we go, wait till I tell you, now listen... I tell you who you don't see much of these days... Wearside Jack.'

A little bit close to the bone this one, due to the association with the Yorkshire Ripper investigation. But a little bit of shock comedy never hurt anyone.

'Listen to this, but listen though, eh? I tell you who you don't see much of these days... Lieutenant Pigeon.'

Smashing reference to the 1970s one-hit wonders – manna from heaven for comedy fans of a certain age who enjoy remembering stuff. Maybe Andy should consider coming on stage to the sound of Lieutenant Pigeon's classic hit, 'Mouldy Old Dough'.

'Do you remember when you were a kid and you had the

measles and your mum would leave you at home when she went to the bingo at night and you'd starve to death? Do you remember it? Do you? That were a laugh, weren't it?'

Everyone, EVERYONE can relate to this. If it didn't happen to you, it happened to someone you know. Bittersweet laughs to be had in spades with this masterful gag.

'Wait till I tell you, wait till I tell you this one, WAIT TILL I TELL YOU... You know all that recycling they go on about? On the news? Well, I never know what to put in the recycling bin so I just chuck in anything that I reckon deserves a second chance.'

Very, very good. Perhaps the environmental brigade should take this on board. I'll almost certainly steal this joke for my next sold-out arena tour. Thanks, Andy!

'Ehhhh, ehhhh, ehhhhhhhhhh, what's it like... I mean, listen, what's it like when you're cooking pasta? Sometimes you cook too much, sometimes you don't cook enough, sometimes... you don't cook any!'

Some might say that pasta humour is very much a relic these days and belongs in the nineteeeeen ninetieeeeeeees. But I'd disagree. Andy has brought it bang up to date here.

'Ehhhh, ehhhh, ehhhhhhh, there's this, though, so listen... I bought meself one of those colanders to strain me pasta in... and I'm not even called Colin!'

Colander. Colin. This is the kind of comedy that makes you think as well as laugh. Top marks.

'Ehhhh, ehhhh, what's the deal with all the kinds of pasta? There's fucking loads!'

Like all the best comedy, this is based in truth. Bravo, Mr Dawson!

CONCLUSION: On this evidence, Bob's long, gradual slide towards showbiz obscurity shows no sign of letting up. Andy, on the other hand, can look forward to a glittering career on the stage, if he can avoid premature death due to his horrendous lifestyle, that is.

ANDY'S ALTERNATIVE NAMES

Throughout the history of Athletico Mince, Bob has offered Andy a series of alternative names to be known as during each podcast, with Andy sniffily refusing almost all of them like the ungrateful wretch that he is. Here are some of the best ones... If you use any of these for yourselves and/or a loved one, please contact Mr Bob Mortimer and arrange a payment of £8.

Ronnie Hot Dog	Youssef Night-Time
Papa Coconuts	Ronnie Hotpot
Dr Hot	Mr Huff 'n' Puff
Daddy Spanners	Billy Mystery
Barry Onions	Tasmin Harp
Slow Kenneth	X-Ray Peter
Minty Tits	Breezy Colin
The King of Lidl	Hot Sauce Harry
The Aldi Express	Ronnie Hot Tits
The Netto Warrior	Dipper Sixpence
Mr Park and Ride	Frankie Wholemeal
Buttery Ken	Valerie Simpleton
The Seed Merchant	Jason Bourne
John Cup	Firehawk
Mr Out 'n' About	Brent Hosepipe
Phillipe Starck	Well Done Edward
Johnny Cuddles	Mr Cupcake

Donny Romance

Ramirez Tapestry

Omelette Ron

Gary From Admin

Mr Chinstrap

Frank Molasses

Chilcott Tits

Maureen Clackers

Dave Meal

Mr Conker

Mr Conkers

Conker Ron

The Horse Chestnut

Gas and Tits Man

Mr Bunsen

Town Gas Tommy

Dark Nectar

Ominous Barry

The Evil Coin

Henry Ree

Charlie Buttons

Sausages and Laughter

Tits McPudding

Lady Caramel

Agent Netto

Aldi Worlde

Aldi Best

Aldi President's Men

Aldi King's Horses

Aldi King's Men

A QUIET NIGHT IN WITH STEVE AND ROY

This story is about a year old, from way back in 2016, and it was the last time that Steve McClaren and Roy Hodgson talked to each other. Steve had invited Roy round for a beans-on-toast supper in, and they were sat in the kitchen diner, in a formal setting that the Fat Lass had set out for them, with napkins and what have you. She'd done a massive pan of baked beans for them and about two-dozen slices of toast, so they were sorted for the entire evening.

So Steve and Roy are sat there, chatting away about the Fat Lass's physiotherapy and that – her chest puts a lot of strain on her back, so she has to have quite a lot of physio. It's not a pleasant detail to have to recount but, if she has a tod, it's quite hard for her to reach round... to... wipe herself. She can get a bit stuck in the... folds... down there, so she sometimes has to really strain and, if she's been a bit loose, she gets Steve up.

'Steeeeeeeeeeve... I've finished – can you wipe me?'

Whenever he hears that from upstairs, he takes a dishcloth up and sorts it and it's absolutely fine.

So Steve is at the table, boasting about his new comfort-fit, short-sleeve, light-blue shirt, and the big thing about the story was that he'd found one with breathable holes under the armpits and it had a special polyester resin in it that kept it really cool. Non-iron and temperature-sensitive – the absolute crème de la crème of comfort-fit, short-sleeve shirts.

To prove his point, he turns the heating right up in the house, just to show off the qualities of the shirt. 'I'm fine, Roy,' he said. 'How are you feeling?'

Roy has a loose-fit shirt on – primrose, it was – and he says, 'Never mind your new material, Steve – this is Egyptian cotton. It cost me three hundred pounds and I'm feeling really refreshed. It is warm in here, Steve, but I'm fine.' This pisses Steve off a bit.

Anyway, they go into the lounge after they've had their beans to watch Steve's favourite old *Poirot* episode that he's got on VHS. The Fat Lass has gone upstairs and suddenly the call comes – 'Steeeeeeeeeeeve... I've finished – can you wipe me?' Which, of course, means that Steve has to nip off out of the room.

Meanwhile, Roy is struggling with the heat but he doesn't want to admit it. Steve's shut all the windows and put one of those snake draught excluders across the bottom of the door. Roy sees his chance to get a bit of air, goes over to the snake draught excluder and picks it up to throw it over the settee.

Just as he's at the top of the arc of his throw, it fucking SPEWS everywhere – its full length comes out of it. All over Roy's shirt, all over Roy's face. Of course, as soon as the snake saw Roy, it thought he was a fucking massive owl – a predator.

Steve then comes down with his stinking dishcloth, and there's the snake on the floor, behind the settee, half its original size and panting for dear life. Roy's covered in spew and Steve has no other option but to throw him out of the house.

The pair haven't spoken since.

SIX THINGS BOBBY CHARLTON LIKED TO DO WITH HIS WORLD-CLASS COMBOVER

- Tying a maggot to the end and dipping it in a stream to fish for tiddlers.
- Lassoing stray dogs and handing them over to the council.
- Dipping it in a tin of paint and creating 'modern art' by lashing it off a canvas.
- Spiking it up with hairspray and offering himself to the community as a mobile lightning rod.
- Hauling injured ants out from disaster scenes and transporting them to safety.
- Tethering himself to a lamp post during High Winds Fortnight.

THE ALDERMAN'S TOFFEE

The last time I saw the Alderman was about three weeks ago, when I went up to Teesside for the screening of a charity film – it was about the decline of the steel and coal industry in the North-East.

Of course, there was snacks and that afterwards and the Alderman collared me at the buffet, so we were talking and then, suddenly, he popped a toffee in my top pocket. I said, 'What was that about? What did you do that for?' and I put my hand into my pocket to see what it was. Anyway, he grabbed my hand so I couldn't get it out of my pocket. He's got a big, fat arm and he's strong and I couldn't get my hand out.

So as he'd got hold of my hand, I said, 'What have you put in there, Alderman?' and he said, 'A lovely creamy toffee.' I've got to be honest, I thought, 'God, I want that toffee.' I felt uncomfortable but I didn't half fancy that toffee.

Then he said, 'You want it, don't you? You want it. You want it, don't you?' and I said, 'I do want the toffee, yeah.' So he says, 'Well, in that case, you know what you have to do,' and then, just as he said those words, the Town Clerk and the Mayor and all his cronies all gathered round and started chanting, 'Kiss the Alderman, Kiss the Alderman, Kiss the Alderman.'

The thing was that I really wanted that toffee so I kissed and I kissed and he opened his mouth quite wide and, as he opened it, he released his grip so I was able to slip my hand in and, just as we finished, I pulled the toffee out and him and his cronies disappeared.

So I'd kissed the Alderman and I'd got myself a lovely creamy toffee. He got what he wanted and I got what I wanted. And where's the harm in that?

ANIMAL MAGIC!

Whether it's a fox, a cat or a disorientated capybara, animal invasions are as much a part of football as diving for penalties and players committing abhorrent Saturday-night crimes, so here's a few of our favourites from down the years…

FULHAM v WEST BROM (1966): A match abandoned after the infamous Keith Bell the Sea Monster came up the Thames and poked his head over the stand and into Craven Cottage. After Keith attempted to eat a dozen fans, Jimmy Greaves said, 'I thought I must have been pissed up on booze and hallucinating, but everyone else saw it as well.' Within seconds, the sea monster was dead, shot by comedian and Fulham chairman Tommy Trinder, who was always armed with a crossbow as part of his act.

BARCELONA v ESPANYOL (1987): Fans at this derby match were shocked when a police horse that had been patrolling outside the Nou Camp threw its rider off and broke into the ground. It then stormed the pitch and executed a perfect sliding tackle on Espanyol midfielder Luis Gonzalez. It later transpired that the horse regularly played football with its police officer handlers and fancied a shot at the big time. Within seconds, it was dead, shot by Espanyol president Xabi 'Big Mambo' Chiquita, who then turned the gun on himself.

FC KÖLN v HAMBURG (1977): A match that became known as 'The Invasion of the Worms'. After sixty-two minutes, more than a million worms suddenly popped up from the Köln pitch, engulfing the players, with four of them swallowed whole within seconds. Believed to be the world's biggest organised worm attack, it was all over minutes later, when machine-gun-toting stewards spattered the worms with round after round of bullets. The rest of the players also perished, including Klaus Hilter, known as 'The Greatest Player Who Wasn't'.

SWANSEA CITY v ROTHERHAM (2001): Cyril the Swan is one of the more famous mascots in the modern game, but he'd prefer to forget the day when an actual male swan swooped on to the pitch at the Vetch Field, knocking him to the ground and attacking him sex-style. Cyril managed to reach for a handgun he was carrying and emptied four bullets into the swan. Six months later, he gave birth to eight baby mascots.

REVELATIONS FROM THE SECRET SOCCER SUPERSTAR

The Secret Soccer Superstar is a regular contributor to the Athletico Mince podcast but, as he is touting around for his own book deal, he was loath to share too many of his stunning revelations with us for our own book. But here's a few snippets on the secret world of definitely being a footballer that he was happy to throw our way...

ON INITIATION CEREMONIES: 'When I signed for a certain top Premier League team about fifteen years ago, the initiation ceremony from my new team-mates was the most brutal I'd ever come across. I was forced into a cauldron at gunpoint in the training-ground dressing rooms and then slow-cooked for eight hours along with some vegetables. When my ordeal was over, they made me eat a steaming bowl of my own body soup, with some croutons sprinkled on top. Even though it was a bit self-cannibalistic, it tasted great.'

ON SUPERSTITIONS: 'Players are weird when it comes to pre-match rituals and superstitions. One top striker I played with couldn't go on to the pitch until he'd jammed a fistful of goat's cheese down his underpants. Another insisted on only squawking in a really high-pitched voice during the half-time break, a bit like a seagull.'

ON PERSONAL DENTISTS: 'This might come as something of a surprise to you, but eighty per cent of Premier League players regularly dream that their teeth are too big for their head. You're guaranteed that a dressing-room discussion on any topic will turn to the subject of teeth and dental hygiene within a couple of minutes. We're obsessed – that's just the way it is. As for me, I had my own personal dentist and used to lie on the on the treatment table and get him to give me a scale and polish twenty minutes before kick-off. If it was a cup final, I'd get him to put me a filling in.'

ON AGENTS: 'A lot of people think that a player's agent is only there to deal with contract negotiations and that, but the agent does so much more for you. Like, when you first sign for a new club, you're a stranger in a new town and your agent does loads of stuff to help you settle in. He'll come round and set up your Xbox for you, he'll get you signed up for swimming lessons and, if you're a member of a fan club for your favourite singer or film star, he'll get in touch with them and let them know your new address.

'Your agent can be really helpful if you're being bullied as well. About ten years ago, I signed for one of the top, top Premier League clubs for ten million quid – I was buzzing!

But, whenever I went down to the precinct to buy a comic or some sweets, the big lads who hung around down there used to pick on me, tripping me up and calling me a puff. It was really affecting my form and the boss put me on the bench for a couple of matches.

'Eventually, my agent went down the precinct on his motorbike and he threatened the lads with a crowbar, and they soon backed off. I got my place back in the starting line-up again, and I even got a couple of Man of the Match prizes.'

ON DEALING WITH WEALTH: 'Some top players spend all their money on flash cars, whilst others fritter it away in casinos and betting shops, but one international centre-half who I played alongside spent his cash a little bit differently. He funded a private militia and used them to overthrow the government of a small Central American country. I can't say which one it was, because it might identify him, but he loved it – he said it was like playing a computer simulation game, but for real. He's dead now.'

ON MIDGETS: 'It's a tradition that's died off in recent years but, when I was playing at the top level, most players had their own midget that they could call on twenty four/ seven. We'd get them to come round our houses, dress up as little waiters and bring us food, drink, drugs, whatever we needed. Usually, as the night dragged on, we'd order them to dance for us, or do some low-level escapology. As the craze took hold, there was a shortage of midgets, so more and more players found themselves having to share one

31

between five of or six of them. It was a boom period for the little fellas themselves, though – they'd be raking it in if they could land an exclusivity deal with one of the highest-earning players.'

THE ALDERMAN AND THE SPRINTER

Did you know that the Alderman owns a car dealership up in Stockton? That's not why I'm always up there with him – I go up because we do lots of charity work together for dozy, cack-handed kids.

Anyway, he's got a dealership. It's on a retail park, and he asked me to go up there to help launch a new model that he's flogging. It's like a big van thing, called a Sprinter. The plan was that I'd cut the ribbon and get a photo with the Alderman for the local press and that.

We'd done all of that and I needed to get a train back down South from Darlington, and the Alderman said, 'I'll tell you what, Bob – I'll take you to Darlington and I'll take you in the new Sprinter.'

I thought, 'Well, that's fair enough – he might want a kiss at the end of it, but that's alright.' So we get in the Sprinter and, about halfway there, he pulls off the dual carriageway into a lay-by. 'Here we go,' I think. 'Here we go... let's get it over with.'

So I lean over to the Alderman, you know, to have a kiss and that, and he says, 'NO, ROBERT! HOW DARE YOU, ROBERT! NOT IN A COMPANY VEHICLE, ROBERT! ESPECIALLY THE NEW SPRINTER!' He's gone all red in the face and everything.

Then I realise that I'm not alone – in the back of the Sprinter, there's the Town Clerk, the Head of Social Services, the Head of the Parks Department, all the gang. They all start chanting as well – 'NOT IN THE SPRINTER! NOT IN THE SPRINTER! NOT IN THE SPRINTER!'

So we get out, in the lay-by, and the Alderman's eyes look down towards the registration number, so I read it – it says, 'YM 16 KTA'. They all start chanting, 'YMKTA! YMKTA! YMKTA!' And it means 'You must kiss the Alderman.' I'm not sure what the '16' is for – maybe it's an age-of-consent thing, or it might be the number of times that you're meant to kiss him.

Time's getting on and I don't want to miss my train, so I give him a lovely little kiss. We had a nice kiss – it tasted a bit like those Party Ring biscuits with the icing on, but mixed with a pepperoni pizza sort of flavour as well.

So, in spite of the hold-up, I got on my train. I suppose the only downside was that, because of kissing the Alderman, I really fancied some pizza and they don't sell it on the train, so that brought a sour end to what had been a pretty strange day.

But he got me to my train on time and I got to go in the new Sprinter, so I can't complain.

FOOTBALLERS IN THE WILD (PART ONE)

One of the most popular sections of our podcast is the bit where listeners report in to us with sightings of top players away from their natural footballing habitat. Here's some of our favourites…

ANDER HERRERA sheltering from a storm beneath a giant urban toadstool.

STUART PEARCE at Stonehenge, frantically trying to wipe a chalk penis off one of the runes with good old spit and elbow grease.

SHANE LONG licking a rainbow lollipop as he wearily judges a Pretty Potato competition at his neighbourhood Summer Fayre.

Sunderland youngsters DUNCAN WATMORE and LYNDEN GOOCH following an unaware DAVID MOYES while pretending to be a couple of cavemen.

JAMES TOMKINS at a film convention, staring at a doll of Mr Blonde from *Reservoir Dogs* for over ten minutes.

MARTIN KEOWN in a high-street record store, trying to return a battered sixteen-year-old copy of 'Jack Your Body' by Steve 'Silk' Hurley, claiming that it was an unwanted gift.

SAMIR NASRI alone in a old-fashioned Blackburn pub, giggling loudly and shouting, 'More blue drinks for all of my friends!'

BAKARY SAKO repeatedly squashing a bulldog puppy as he tries to test-ride it around a dog showroom.

BRENDAN RODGERS and a small boy with a heavily bandaged face whom Rodgers had strapped into a wheel-barrow. The pair were trying to sell advertising space on the boy's bandages to confused passers-by.

DENNIS BERGKAMP trying on false moustaches in a Holloway Road joke shop. He finally settled for the 'Sloppy Drooper'.

ROY KEANE at a charity auction, bidding furiously for a copy of *Last Exit To Brooklyn* as soiled by the author. He dropped out at £29.50.

WILLIAN ingratiating himself with the locals in Chelsea's 'Fishnets' restaurant by standing on a table and bawling an Anglo-Portuguese version of 'There Must Be an Angel (Playing With My Heart)'.

TROY DEENEY driving a motorised bed down the street in aid of a charity for orphaned clowns.

SALOMÓN RONDÓN knocking on random doors, offering strangers tarot readings from a pack of *Knight Rider* Top Trumps he was carrying with him.

YANNICK BOLASIE rifling through a skip, looking for used tubes of arse cream.

ALAN PARDEW looking at himself in a shard of broken mirror that he'd picked up in a car park, and muttering, 'You're either part of the solution or you're part of the problem, Alan.'

Everton trio LEIGHTON BAINES, SEAMUS COLEMAN and PHIL JAGIELKA playing at being Charlie's Angels in a packed Liverpool bar.

HARRY REDKNAPP on a scouting holiday to Cuba, throwing melons at unsuspecting young men in a bid to judge their reflexes.

Swansea midfielder JACK CORK on the town with his new love, Zelda from *Terrahawks*.

Opening his own parsley farm near Urmston, Manchester United's DALEY BLIND.

MARK HUGHES on the platform of Newark train station, dressed as Sweeney Todd and combing the hair of waiting passengers for a guinea a time.

Chelsea gaffer ANTONIO CONTE parading through The Oratory in a coat made from cooked pasta shells.

Seen in the German town of Koblenz, GAËL CLICHY pretending to sneeze but actually saying the word 'Nazis'.

STEWART DOWNING digging up part of the hard shoulder on the A19 and putting a plastic sheep in the hole.

PETR CECH (without his trademark sex hat) returning a Pacman costume to a hire shop and trying to explain away what he described as 'mayonnaise stains'.

MICHAEL CARRICK dressed as Santa Claus, refusing to give a urine sample, saying, 'Santa don't do smack, baby.'

RYAN GIGGS decorating the exterior of his mock-mock-

Tudor mansion with a massive luminous turkey on a pendulum, swinging slowly back and forth across the front of the house.

JAMIE VARDY barking with glee as his barber rubs fake snow into his scalp and beard area.

In Queens Gardens, Hull City boss MIKE PHELAN down to his last £50 after losing everything in a poker game with club mascot Rory the Tiger.

Off the Spanish coast, former World Cup winner GEOFF HURST swimming naked with dolphins and telling them, in dolphin language, about how he won the World Cup in 1966.

Asleep in a wheelbarrow, wearing a suit of autumn leaves, LEON OSMAN.

GARETH BARRY pouring a large bag of salt onto a playground snowman while singing Kanye West's 'Gold Digger'.

Celtic's LEIGH GRIFFITHS setting up an illegal shortbread factory in Glasgow.

Chelsea owner ROMAN ABRAMOVICH sitting on DAVID LUIZ'S back and shouting, 'Faster donkey, faster!'

Middlesbrough's NEGREDO cutting out a length of carpet under a railway bridge in County Durham.

RYAN SHAWCROSS getting PETER CROUCH to reach into a tree to rescue CHARLIE ADAM'S stuck kite.

KASPER SCHMEICHEL driving a steamroller over some china models of Louis Walsh in that car park in Leicester.

AITOR KARANKA commanding the Middlesbrough academy players to 'build me a mausoleum that will make the Pyramids look like mere toys.'

ROBBIE SAVAGE destroying the livelihood of an entire Inuit tribe in Greenland.

Hull City striker ABEL HERNANDEZ performing an experimental poetry show, 'Larkin to Parkin', at Spring Street Theatre in Hull.

Spurs gaffer MAURICIO POCHETTINO urging his team to dance for him 'like the girls of my homeland.'

MESUT ÖZIL affecting a yawn at a poster of Brad Pitt in HMV, and saying, 'Seen it all before, beauty boy.'

West Ham boss SLAVEN BILIC bellowing, 'Let's do *Murder She Wrote*. I'll be Angela Lansbury,' at a collection of bemused players.

A TOP HAT FULL OF WORMS lying outside Coventry's Ricoh Arena.

ROBERT HUTH at a garden centre near Darlington, licking an assortment of trees.

The entire CRYSTAL PALACE squad carrying out a team-building exercise by recreating an episode of *Cracker*, with the part of the burly sleuth being played by a padded-up CONNOR WICKHAM.

LEE CATTERMOLE trying to talk a badly injured rabbit into dying naturally as he tied it to his head to use as a hat.

MAX GRADEL paying a groonup of passing schoolchildren £40 each to form a human pyramid, in order to support his legs while he did his first ever handstand.

An angry ARSÈNE WENGER outside the headquarters of eBay, complaining about some soggy fireworks he claimed to have bought from them.

RAFA BENITEZ trying to coax a twitching, frightened wig out of a tree with a low-pitched incantation.

JOHN TERRY in a café, cutting out all the 'g's from a copy of the *Daily Express* and eating them.

THEO WALCOTT in a record shop, asking for a CD that's 'like jazz, only more quiet.'

MARK LAWRENSON – PEST CONTROLLER

I've had such a lucky break because I've found someone who's got a contact who can give me all the gossip about Mark Lawrenson. So here goes…

You might not know this but he's got a real passion for pest control. He doesn't like football all that much but he loves pest control and dabbles in it a bit in his spare time. He's got a brother-in-law who does it, and Mark always wishes he'd gone into the business instead of becoming a footballer.

Michael Owen phoned him up recently and asked him if he'd do a pest check on his new restaurant in Manchester before it opened up for its press night. It's a beautiful place – a great big old Georgian building. Used to be part of the zoo in Manchester, apparently – massive place, ideal for a posh restaurant.

Anyway, Michael wanted it checked out for pests because, if there was anything wrong, he didn't want it getting in the papers, and he knew he could trust Mark to be discreet if he found anything.

So Mark turns up with all his kit – he's got traps, sprays, sticky sheets, goggles, those gloves that go right up to your neck, all the gear. Top-notch pest-controller kit. He goes into the kitchen, because that's the main area to check, puts on the lights and, just as he does, he thinks he sees a massive bloke scuttle off out through the fire exit. He thinks it was probably a homeless fella on the rob or something, and doesn't really give it a second thought.

Then he gets on with all the checks he has to do – he

41

checks the cookers, all the nooks and crannies, looking for droppings, eggs, all that sort of stuff, all the tell-tale signs for pests. He's looking for roaches, ants, mice droppings – he's come prepared and he's got a massive checklist. The only things he finds is a little bit of thick brown hair and quite a lot of large, dirty boot-sized footprints – that's more of an Environmental Health thing but he thinks he'll tell Michael anyway.

There are a couple of other things near the door – a great big pile of quite dark tod and a bit of blood smeared on the floor, but he just assumes that it's from the homeless bloke. Food-wise, the only thing untoward that he sees is an open jar of honey on one of the work surfaces. Obviously, he tells Michael about the honey and the blood and the footprints and the tod but, pest-wise, he's able to give it a 100 per cent clean bill of health.

They're having a little chat after he's gives it the all-clear, and he asks Michael what he's going to call the new restaurant, because he sees that the signwriters have arrived. Michael says that he's going to call it 'Mo's', because the 'M' and 'O' are the same as his initials.

Mark says, 'Hey, Michael, don't call it that. For one thing, it's like the bar in *The Simpsons*, and that's fun but this is going to be a really serious, upmarket restaurant and a name like that will give off the wrong kind of vibe.

'Second, I'm a bit worried that it's like a short form of "motherfucker", like "mofo", and I don't like that, Michael.'

Michael panics and says, 'Shit, I don't know, Mark – it's a bit late in the day to change it. The sign writers are here, the menus are printed.'

Mark replies, 'Come on, Michael, we can sort this in half an hour – the name's going to stick forever. It needs to be a name that sums up you – you know, your essence. What do you believe in, Michael? What do you stand for?'

Michael says, 'I don't know really. I like helicopters, I like Dubai, I like leather furniture, I like betting, I like me side parting...'

Mark angrily interrupts him, saying, 'Michael, man – honestly. When I think of you, I think of inspiration, integrity, style, sophistication – use those words, use them somehow in your restaurant name. Anyway, it's a hundred quid for the pest thing, and don't forget to clean that stuff up in the kitchen.'

It's press night in the restaurant later on – all the paparazzi are there. Rio Ferdinand, Gary Barlow, Dynamo the magician, Lizzie Cundy, Ken Morley and Razor Ruddock are all there. A-listers. Michael stands in front of the big restaurant window, ready to unveil the curtain.

He proudly says, 'Ladies and gentlemen, my restaurant stands for inspiration, sophistication, integrity and style. So here goes – I pronounce the restaurant *open!*' He pulls down the curtain and there in massive letters is I... S... I... S.

ISIS.

He's called his restaurant ISIS.

There's a big intake of breath and the cameras start flashing. 'No!' says Michael. 'It's inspiration, sophistication, integrity and style, it's not the terrorist thingy.' Just as he's speaking, the window smashes to pieces, and out runs a fucking great big brown bear. It roars, it sniffs the air, runs straight at Gary Barlow and punches him in his tits before disappearing into the back streets of Didsbury.

Think about it – the big black pile of tod, the honey – all the tell-tale signs were there. Mark's messed up big time. He's looked at the smaller detail, the droppings and stuff, and he's missed the bigger picture. He thinks he's an expert in the pest-control business and he's missed a fucking bear.

It was a terrible night for Michael and for the entire Manchester restaurant clique, not to mention Mark's reputation. He gave up on the pest-control thing for a while after that.

45

A HISTORY
OF FOOTBALL

PART TWO
THE SEVENTIES

May 1970: Luton Town midfielder and born-again Christian Peter Logan loses his appeal to play matches with an inflatable representation of God on his shoulders. Logan retires from football with immediate effect and vows to devote his life to creating a packet of crisps that only taste nice if you believe in Jesus.

November 1970: Austrian club FC Wistleblauer sign up the mother of their star strikers Wolfgang and Dieter Holtz, with plans to use her as a footballing breeding machine. Frau Holz lives in a palatial apartment in the town and is visited twice daily by current and retired Austrian legends as they attempt to create a new race of superstars. However, Frau Holtz is sixty-three and the only child she gives birth to is Walter, a slow-witted son with webbed feet and a combover to cover his scabby, balding head.

June 1971: The FA steps in after Preston North End attempt to take their players away on a themed end-of-season trip – hunting down and slaying the Tranmere Rovers squad. North End boss Billy Astle says, 'Some people have suggested it's just sour grapes after Rovers pipped us to the last promotion place in the very last minute of the final match of the season, but that's madness. Individually pursuing and eliminating their entire squad would have been a valuable team-building exercise for us. We just chose a set of targets that we had recent experience of. It's all perfectly innocent.'

October 1971: Middlesbrough have a request to postpone their match with Bristol Rovers turned down by the FA, after their excuse of 'We forgot to practise' isn't deemed worthy of postponement.

February 1972: Plans are announced to commemorate Grimsby and Burnley's recent eleven-goal thriller in the form of a tapestry. The match, which Grimsby won 6-5, was hailed as the highlight of both clubs' recent history and, therefore, worthy of an extravagant cloth tribute.

The planned tapestry will be 100m long upon completion (which is expected to be in the spring of 1980) and will include recreations of each of the goals, along with flattering close-ups of match referee Ted Cochrane.

The two clubs say they will split the cost of the tapestry, believed to be around £1.5 million, and are to undertake self-imposed transfer embargoes for the next eight years in order to pay for it. It is believed that more than two hundred semi-retired weavers will be employed to construct it.

June 1972: Crystal Palace defender Roy Penistone reveals that he knew his days at the club were numbered when he lost the privilege of taking the club's wolf home at weekends. Players take it in turns to look after the wolf, named Django, and Penistone says his name was scribbled out on the rota at the last minute twice in recent weeks. He told us, 'It didn't surprise me. The management knew how close I was to that wolf and splitting us up was the final straw.'

Penistone is said to have been revitalised by his move to Fulham, who have recently added a zebra and a eunuch to their menagerie.

October 1972: York-based confectioners, Terry's, ride the wave of 1970s soccer superstardom and introduce a line of football figurines made out of fudge. Among the personalities available are Dennis Law (toffee), Bryan 'Pop' Robson (clotted cream) and Derek Dougan (rum 'n' raisin).

December 1972: Carlisle United bosses are criticised after trying something a bit different for their half-time entertainment during a home FA Cup tie against Aldershot Town. The sight of local asylum seekers wearing oversized face masks of former *Blue Peter* presenters parading around the pitch perimeter is regarded by some as not suitable for a family football match, mainly due to the nudity.

April 1973: The last ever black-and-white game is played as West Ham meet Everton in the final game of the season. Traditionally, all matches had been played in monochrome, with all players and fans decked out in various shades of grey, to match television pictures.

But as colour television becomes more popular, everyone is allowed to start sporting their club's colours, and black-and-white football is finally phased out for good.

July 1973: The transfer record in the South Berkshire Over-40 League Division 3 is shattered for the second time in as many weeks, when Tommy Boulter is transferred from The Griffin Inn to The Snitch and Weasel for an amazing 95p and a hairnet that used to belong to Barbara Windsor. Only a few days earlier, The Griffin had bought Ron Kellogg from The Draymen Reserve XI for a snapped guitar string and a mug filled with soot. Fans fear that the non-league transfer market will soon spiral out of control.

December 1973: Burnley fan Simon Hepplestone is believed to be the first supporter to be capable of flight. The forty-two-year-old ironmonger has super-glued feathers to his body and claims he flies to away matches. However, rivals and sceptics say that he makes his way to and from matches not through the skies but in his Ford Cortina and, after an inquiry, he is stripped of his FA aviation funding.

May 1974: River Plate defender Diego Manusco makes a record eight hundred and sixty-second appearance as an unused substitute. But he has used his match-day time creatively, writing a series of short stories that have bewitched the club's president, Hugo Moretti.

Manusco insists that he has been happy warming the bench and that it has been the perfect place for his creativity to shine through, saying, 'When I am at home, I am easily distracted by the television or the urge to polish my collection of brass parakeets. Only when I am on the touchline does my imagination begin to soar, like my parakeets, except real ones and not ones that have been fashioned from brass.'

President Moretti insists that Manusco is picked as a substitute for every match from 1962 until 1974, happily paying the player £5,000 just to write stories while the games go on. The stocky full-back's tales are predominantly about a time-travelling brass salesman and his loyal parakeet sidekick.

June 1974: Seventy thousand cans of Irn Bru are withdrawn from sale after it is revealed that they can pick up live World Cup action for free if placed on top of an ordinary TV. The discovery is made by Scotland fan Jim Bodie, when he puts his can down on top of the telly in order to carry out a particularly complicated and drawn-out fart. Jim appears in a local paper with his story and the cans are withdrawn at once, before Irn Bru chiefs realise that the World Cup matches are all on TV anyway and that the cans have no special powers.

July 1974: Zaire are knocked out of the World Cup finals when their 'human shield' tactic fails them in a penalty shoot-out. The Africans draw each of their group games 0-0 by having ten 6ft 5in players standing in a row on their goal line, with an 8ft man lying across their heads. For the penalty shoot-out in round two, they wheel on their sub keeper, a 65st man who almost fills the entire goal. Unfortunately, he wanders off when he sees someone with a hot dog, and the match is lost.

October 1974: Frank Worthington and his Leicester City team-mate Keith Weller have a public falling-out over Worthington's habit of wearing a Stetson cowboy hat before matches, which Weller continually and incorrectly refers to as a 'stentson'. The dispute is eventually settled by a duel in the car park at Filbert Street, which Worthington wins when he shoots Weller in the thigh.

December 1974: A new survey has revealed that 66 per cent of British schoolchildren want Manchester City forward Rodney Marsh for Christmas. The favoured reason among girls is 'because he's cute', while boys voted for the England international as an ideal gift 'because he's a fast runner.' Marsh's manager, Tony Book, says, 'For the last time, Rodney is going nowhere.'

March 1975: A new format of indoor football, known as Speed Soccer, is launched, with a high-profile tournament taking place at Wembley's Empire Pool including all of the top First Division clubs. Sadly, it is deemed a failure – each match lasts for just three seconds, and the tournament has no winner after an unending string of 0-0 results.

June 1975: Furious Barnsley fans react to the sale of star striker Kenny Bishop to Spurs for a paltry £60,000 by dismantling the club's Oakwell ground. As the news of the transfer breaks, hundreds of fans converge on the ground to register their disgust, but the protest soon turns nasty when one fan rips away an exit gate. Others quickly join in and, within two hours, the entire ground has been taken apart and whisked away in lorries. The fans only return the thousands of parts of the stadium when the Barnsley board agree to scrap the transfer of Bishop.

July 1975: The FA introduce new rules over the use of touchline advertising by managers. For the past five months, flamboyant Crystal Palace manager Malcolm Allison has been seen in the dugout blowing out the word 'Esso' in cigar smoke, which has prompted the authorities to clamp down on illicit advertising techniques. England boss Don Revie is said to be livid, as he has just finished constructing a sandwich board with 'EAT PORK PRODUCTS' daubed on it.

January 1976: Non-league Brayton Wanderers continue their dismal run of eleven straight league defeats after their chairman imposed an overtime ban. Skipper Mike Hopper says, 'It's out of our control. Because of the ban, once ninety minutes is up, we're under orders to leave the field. Unfortunately, we've let in a few crucial goals as a result.' Their most recent 15-4 defeat came after the side were seemingly cruising with a 3-0 lead at the 90-minute mark. Defender Scott Coppell, who defied the rule and stayed on alone to score a fourth, has had his contract terminated.

October 1976: Middlesbrough have a request to postpone their match with Bristol Rovers turned down by the FA, after their excuse of 'We don't think the opposition are going to turn up – don't ask us why, it's just a hunch' isn't deemed worthy of postponement.

February 1977: Ipswich Town midfielder Ian Hedge announces his retirement from the game at the age of twenty-four, owing to a persistently itchy leg.

March 1977: Leicester midfielder Keith Hobbs is transfer-listed by the club after it is discovered he has been feigning injury and missing training for five weeks. Hobbs had been spending his time in his garage making short films with a cine camera and submitting them to BBC1 children's show *Screen Test* in an illegal bid to win their 'Young Film Maker of the Year' award. He said, 'I'm just an amateur so I said I was eight years old. I never thought I'd win, though.' But Hobbs is wrong and his short film of four ducks on a lake who amazingly disappear into thin air is declared the best in its age category, only for him to be stripped of the trophy once the truth emerges.

August 1977: Instead of the usual press conference, Everton's new signing, and notorious wide-boy, Stan Leamington decides he'll mark his arrival by parachuting into the centre circle at Goodison. Five hundred fans turn up but, unknown to Leamington, his agent secures a better deal with Liverpool at the last minute and calls off the transfer. As the player descends into Goodison, he is greeted with a hail of rocks, bottles and engine parts, and misses the entire season with his horrifying injuries.

October 1977: York City terminate the contract of midfielder Roy Kent after he only manages to complete eleven minutes on the pitch in a total of eleven matches, falling foul of a red card for violent conduct after approximately a minute in every match he plays. 'It's not working out for the lad or for us,' says manager Bob Carter.

March 1978: Stoke City's fight for survival receives a boost after it is announced that an angle-poise lamp will take the place of midfielder David Blight for the remainder of the season. Blight has been told to stay away from the Victoria Ground until his contract expires in the summer, and the lamp, which is ferried around on a trolley, becomes a noticeable presence at the club. An unnamed player tells the *Stoke Sentinel*, 'The lamp is usually in the corner of the dressing room before matches and it's definitely brightens things up. Dave was becoming a bit boring, so maybe it's the spark we need.' Updated posters of the season's squad photo, which have the tough-tackling midfielder replaced by the forty-watt lamp, are available for fans and quickly sell out.

May 1978: Ecuador coach Hector Paz prepares his players for the forthcoming Argentina World Cup finals by putting them through their paces with his new 'lightning machine'. Made from a giant umbrella and powered by his bicycle, Paz's contraption strikes his players with powerful bolts of lightning whenever he pedals fast enough. The Ecuador players are disgruntled by the training sessions, as incidents of lightning strikes in Argentina are extremely rare. They are also unhappy as they haven't actually qualified for the finals, and just want to go on holiday with their wives and families.

July 1978: The West End show *Gerry Francis: The Opera* closes after just four days, in the wake of scores of complaints. The Crystal Palace midfielder, who wrote and starred in the production, said, 'I've no real regrets, but maybe I included a bit too much stuff about pigeon-fancying.' A spokesman for the Lyric Theatre, where it was performed, adds, 'Sixteen hundred pigeons perished during that show. That's not what we call entertainment round here.'

October 1978: Eyebrows are raised when ex-Ajax star Jordi Van Der Pfeffen opts to sign for middling FC Schalke. But the Dutch international clarifies his reasons for the decision, telling us, 'I am the number-one Rolling Stones fan, and I plan to draw their hot-tongue logo across Europe with my career moves. Next stop: Stranraer!' Indeed, his surname Van Der Pfeffen translates as 'of the tongue'.

February 1979: Carlisle United bosses are criticised after trying something a bit different for their half-time entertainment during a home FA Cup tie against Accrington Stanley. The sight of highly acclaimed performance-art duo Flux & Constant miming the crossing of the River Styx on the pitch, finishing up among fans in the Warwick Road End, is regarded by some as not suitable for a family football match, mainly due to the nudity.

April 1979: An unsuccessful penalty appeal by Lincoln City during a crucial match with Stockport County continues well after the final whistle, going on for a full five days after the incident. Striker Barry Dodds claimed he was tripped in the box in injury time, and was furious when referee Roger Bishop failed to award the spot kick. Dodds lambasted the official as the teams left the field, and even followed Bishop home, spending the rest of the weekend hammering on the referee's window and shouting through his letterbox.

The on-loan striker refused to give up, haranguing Bishop's children as they left for school on Monday, and then tailing the official as he left for his day job as a marketing manager.

A shabby and unshaven Dodds, who had been sleeping in a hedge in Bishop's garden, is forced to end his marathon penalty appeal when he is tranquillised in the face.

October 1979: Conjoined twins and Belgian midfielders Wesley and Joos Clement take FIFA to court after the governing body say they count as two players, rather than one, even though the twins are joined at the neck and only have one body between them. FIFA say that their two heads give them an added advantage during matches, but the pair insist that only Wesley is interested in football and that Joos wants to be a country-and-western singing star instead. An agreement is eventually reached and the pair are allowed to compete as just one player, but Joos must wear a sack over his head and a gag in his mouth during matches.

STEVE'S SPECIAL VISITOR

In the week when Big Sam Allardyce was appointed as England manager, he got in touch with Steve McClaren so that he could pick his brains about the sort of things he might come up against in the job.

Big Sam rang up and said, 'Can I come round and have a chat about stuff to do with the England job?' so Steve invited him round to the house. The trouble is that the Fat Lass has always had a thing about Sam, so Steve isn't really all that keen on having him round.

As soon as the Fat Lass found out Big Sam was coming round, she was all, like, 'Shall we have a barbecue?' She knew that, if she just did the classic beans on toast in the kitchen, Steve would just say, 'Right, that's great, thanks love. Off you go,' and she wouldn't get to be around Sam. But the garden is accessible, so she knew she'd be able to flit about and chat with Sam, which was exactly what she wanted.

They go outside for the barbecue and Steve shows Big Sam his vegetable plot. 'There's my tomatoes, spuds, peas and all that' – he's quite proud of it. But the Fat Lass is hovering about and she's got a great big pan of baked beans and a load of toast, and what's she's done is, she's pierced the toast on to Steve's samurai sword that he keeps above his bath.

She said, 'Here's a fun starter, Steve – I put some toast on your sword,' and there's about thirty-eight pieces of toast impaled on it. She didn't give them a knife and fork, just a wooden spoon each, because she reckons that's a good, fun outdoor way to eat your baked beans.

Anyway, Sam says, 'So, tell us about this England job,' and Steve tells him all about his experience. Meanwhile, the Fat Lass has been drinking those coffee martinis and she's a bit tipsy on them, so she goes inside, gets Steve's yellow snake, Casper, and starts doing a sort of fat dance with him on the lawn. You know, like a sort of belly dance.

To cut a long story short, she ends up collapsing with the coffee martinis – Casper nips off into the vegetable patch and she's just lying there on the grass, prostrate. About twenty minutes later, Steve says, 'Sam, go and pick us a corn cob and we'll throw it on the barbecue, eh?'

Sam goes into the vegetable patch, sees the yellow gleaming there among the foliage, tugs at it... you've guessed it: it's not a corn cob, it's Casper. The snake opens his eyes, stares straight at Sam, thinks he's looking at a bear, and spews up while Sam's got hold of him.

It was quite a funny one for Steve, because Sam was holding Casper facing upwards and the spew came up and down again, all the way across to the prostrate Fat Lass, who was still lying sparked out on the lawn. An arc of spew.

It soaked the Fat Lass and, because she's in love with Sam, she was so upset that he saw her like that, so she rushed upstairs, mortified. Later that night, after Sam had gone, Steve put their favourite *Poirot* VHS tape on for her and he put it on loud, so she could hear it upstairs, but she didn't come down. She didn't come down.

JEREMY CORBYN'S TATTOO CHALLENGE

I was up in Inverness last week, at a Jeremy Corbyn rally. As usual, I was in the mosh pit, getting up close and personal, trying to breathe in some of that vapour of raw charisma that he gives off. He did quite a short set – a few cover versions of Billy Bragg songs. Twenty minutes, on and off, no interval and no encore. Quite reminiscent of an early Jesus & Mary Chain gig.

Afterwards, I went round the back because I was gasping for a fag. Sure enough, out comes Corbyn – he pulls out his pipe, stuffs some foul-smelling tobacco into it and sparks it up. He looks across at me. 'Seen you,' he says. 'Seen you. Down the front. Tapping your foot. Think you're a bit of a mover and a groover, don't you?' And, you know, I like to dance – always have done – so I reply, 'Yeah, that was me.'

So he says, 'How many tattoos have you got, laddie?' Well, I haven't got any – I'm not really into tattoos. I think it's weird, but each to their own, so I just said, 'I haven't got any, for what it's worth.' Trying to be diplomatic and non-committal, because I wasn't completely sure where he was going with this. Corbyn sniffed and said, 'Nnnn, you look the type. Ask me my best tattoo. Go on, ask me my best one.'

So I said, 'What's your best tattoo, Jeremy?'

'Hammer and sickle. Just above my arse. Do you know why it's my best?'

'Not really,' I said. Wasn't sure if I even wanted to know.

He says, 'Because it hurt the most.'

Now, I don't understand tattoo culture; I don't understand why anyone would disfigure their body like that. I'm pretty much a perfect specimen myself – why blight this flawless canvas? But, like I say, each to their own.

So Corbyn just sneers at me. 'Come back when you've got yourself inked... AND NOT A FUCKING HENNA ONE EITHER. REAL INK.'

He was starting to get a bit aggressive at that point. Luckily, John McDonnell, the Shadow Chancellor, pulled up on a motorbike, Corbyn got in the sidecar and off they went.

Don't think I'll be taking him up on his offer.

CELEBRITY CHADWICKS

Bob recently asked some of his showbiz pals to weigh their chadwicks, and here's the results!

(Figures rounded up to nearest tenth of a gram.)

17 g – Trevor Nelson
16.7 g – Alfie Boe
16.5g – Dame Shirley Bassey
16.5 g – Dave from Chas & Dave
16.2 g – Mary J Blige
16 g – Olly Murs
15.8 g – Jimmy Tarbuck
15.3 g – Linda Robson
15.2 g – Darcey Bussell
15.2 g – Andrea Bocelli
15 g – Biffy Clyro
14.4 g – Heather Mills

14.1 g – Tony Bennett
14 g – Adele
13.3 g – Myleene Klass
13.1 g – Craig Revel Horwood
12.8 g – The cast of *Wicked* (average weight)
12.2 g – Ozzy Osbourne
11.7 g Natasha Kaplinsky
11.1 g – Donny Osmond
7.3 g – Charlotte Church
4.1 g – Chris Evans

FOOTBALLERS IN THE WILD (PART TWO)

Here's more of our favourite player sightings from the Footballers in the Wild section of the Athletico Mince podcast.

ADAM LALLANA holding a robot's head underwater in the River Mersey, shouting, 'Now THAT'S an oxbow lake, you tin-minded bastard!'

JOSÉ MOURHINO discussing the ingredients of a shepherd's pie with a bored-looking publican.

CHRIS BRUNT strapped into a hang glider and trying to take off from the roof of his Jeep.

YOUNÈS KABOUL being cornered by deranged juvenile fans offering him their used chewing gum in Watford High Street.

DAVID MOYES reading the poetry of Robert Burns for cash, to nobody whatsoever, on the defunct set of TV's *Brookside*.

CLAUS LUNDEKVAM scrubbing off the phrase 'Snake

Charmer', which had been daubed in paint on the front of his house for the umpteenth time.

KEVIN KILBANE crouched behind a knoll, throwing conkers at a Green Flag mechanic he had lured into position with a hoax call.

WILFRIED BONY and DAVID SILVA sitting in a deserted children's playground, surrounded by a pile of £50 notes, betting on which of them can first cry a thimbleful of their own tears.

DANNY MURPHY tripping in the street before repeating the motion a number of times as if it was deliberate.

DIMITRI PAYET visiting the set of *Coronation Street* and banging on the door of No.1, yelling, 'Ken! Ken! Come out. I am here to see you!'

LOUIS VAN GAAL spending a week's leave sailing up a Vietnamese river in search of a mythical centre-half.

GORDON STRACHAN in full Harlequin make-up, teaching his pet seal, Gemini, to balance a ball on its nose.

JONJO SHELVEY pouring coins into a *Bananas in Pyjamas* children's ride at a motorway service station, shouting, 'Forty-five minutes on the bucking bronco! Come on!'

A shivering JUAN MATA at a car-boot sale, selling graphic novels based on the film *Jumanji* that he had individually drawn himself on rolls of toilet paper.

JURGEN KLINSMANN demanding a refund from the guided tour of the *Emmerdale* set because he claimed it was smaller than it looked on TV.

GARY CAHILL performing onstage with his new yuletide-based sex-funk group Toxic Tinsel.

DANNY INGS hauling a burned-out dragon carcass down the middle of the road.

STEVE BRUCE dishing out a car-park haranguing to Aston Villa's new aromatherapist over some rancid jasmine.

JACK WILSHERE chasing a gang of skate-punks who had been repeatedly calling him 'Wilf'.

CLAUDIO RANIERI forcing his Leicester forwards to practise free kicks using a giant harp as a dummy wall.

FERNANDO LLORENTE recovering from injury by sitting at a bus stop and trying to impress girls by burning holes in his arm with a cigarette.

HEURELHO GOMES advertising inflammable screwdrivers on a digital shopping channel.

PATRICK BAMFORD in his car, crying as he read a Minette Walters novel.

JERMAINE JENAS at his local deed-poll centre, asking how much it would cost to change his name to 'Jimmy Genius'.

GASTON RAMIREZ standing in the middle of Middlesbrough town centre with his arms raised above his head and yelling up into the sky, 'Will somebody please tell me what is going on?'

ROBERT SNODGRASS grabbing a terrified pensioner and asking if he could squeeze his zits for him.

NEIL WARNOCK behind the decks at an Essex warehouse party, spinning grooves under his pseudonym 'DJ Evil Horse'.

TREVOR BROOKING whimpering, 'I want my mammy,' after being scared by a clown having an epileptic fit in Oxford Circus.

LIONEL MESSI sulking after being told he couldn't wear his new trainers on the flight back from Barcelona's match with Real Mallorca.

JOHN MIKEL OBI straining his face in an attempt to grow a speed-beard before Chelsea's annual Frank Zappa lookalike contest.

FABIAN DELPH clambering out of a manhole with a copy of Will Self's *The Book of Dave* clenched between his teeth.

PETER CROUCH and a gang of midgets dressed as Sneezy the Dwarf, delivering an anti-hay-fever petition to 10 Downing Street.

JERMAIN DEFOE sitting alone in a Wimpy, practising his kissing on the back of his hand.

KEVIN KILBANE in the middle of Iran, washing his face in a frying pan.

DARL JANMAAT throwing himself in front of the King's horse at Cheltenham as a protest against the Suffragettes.

A quivering CRAIG GARDNER putting a banger into a deep-fried Mars Bar before lighting it and watching it explode.

BAKARY SAKO redeeming a balloon voucher, as given to him by his team-mates for his birthday.

WILLY CABALLERO in the Manchester City club shop, being shown how to work the till.

Arsenal's CARL JENKINSON and DAVID OSPINA riding a tandem down by the Emirates Stadium in the middle of the night.

Fat RONALDO (the Brazilian one) in a wheelchair in Cardiff, staring vacantly into the window of Ann Summers while his helper scratched his back for him with a knitting needle.

RYAN GIGGS in a phone box, ringing up to order a skip for his house. He said he had loads of red stuff he wanted to get rid of.

RIYAD MAHREZ at Heathrow Airport with a carrier bag full of sweets and a cowboy hat that he was wearing at a jaunty angle. He was offering the sweets to strangers and saying they were 'painkillers'. He bought himself a one-way ticket to Munich.

ROBBIE KEANE painting a cow red and white in a field on the outskirts of Sunderland.

ROY KEANE in Corfu, with a tattoo of a spider's web on his face. There's a Newcastle United magpie in the web, and Keane was drinking Brown Ale non-stop.

MAMADOU SAHKO outside Anfield, counting the turnstiles and writing stuff down in a notebook.

DAVID SILVA in a taxi at Glasgow Airport, asking to see the spot where John Smeaton punched that burning terrorist. Then he got out and started doing kung-fu kicks.

DIMITAR BERBATOV in a nightclub in Ilford, hassling the DJ to play 'Part of the Union' by The Strawbs.

ANDY COLE paddling in the sea at Blackpool while wearing a 'Kiss Me Quick' hat and sucking hard on some candy floss.

PHIL JONES parked next to the sign that says 'Welcome to Burnley' at the entrance to the town, before getting out of his car and kissing it.

EMMANUEL EBOUÉ outside Upton Park, boxing with his own shadow while some kids cheered him on.

MARCUS RASHFORD sailing up the River Irwell on a rickety looking pirate ship.

JOEY BARTON stood outside Wandsworth Prison, stopping passers-by and forcefully saying, 'Don't know what that is, never even heard of it. Definitely never been to prison, me.'

VIRGIL VAN DIJK's mum in a launderette, washing his Southampton kit, telling a stranger that he's getting her a helicopter for Christmas.

GANGS OF THE EPL – THE SPURS GANG

I went to the Riverside the other week for the Middlesbrough v Tottenham match; we were a bit out of our depth against them. So I go up into hospitality lounge afterwards while the traffic outside clears – and I go to the toilet.

In there is Debbie Alli, Harry Kane and Eric Dier, and they're all wearing tight black, thin polo necks, tight black, skinny trousers and pointy black shoes. I was a bit startled and I stood still, looking at them.

So Harry Kane says, 'What do you want? This is a private club for Spurs players,' and then Debbie Alli says, 'Yeah, and even if you're a Spurs player, you have to have the right club clothes on.' Then Eric Dier says, 'And even if you're Spurs with the right clothes on, you have to know the secret club password.'

So I said, 'Well, it's 'Come on, you Spurs' – and they all looked really fucked off. Debbie Alli says, 'How did you know?' then Harry says, 'We were going to change it anyway so you can fuck off,' and I said, 'Alright, I'm not bothered what you get up to – I mean, what do you actually do in this club?'

Debbie says, 'We look in the mirror mostly,' and Harry says, 'Yeah, and we sit in each other's cars.' Eric says, 'Go shopping, Snapchat quite a lot too,' and I pretended and said, 'Oh yeah, that sounds like really good fun, that, lads. Well done to you lot, "Come on, you Spurs" and all that.'

Anyway, at this point, bang – the door opens behind me – in comes Toby Alderweireld and Vans Vertonghen. They stroll in, both of them wearing Robin Hood green tracksuits and trilbies, and they start yodelling. 'YODELAY-LO-LAY-LO-LO-HO-YO!'

Harry Kane, with an angry look on his face, says 'Get out! This is our clubhouse! We were here first!' Toby says, 'We are older than you so we say what happens around here! You might like to check your birth certificate or ask your mam, 'cos that's what we did.'

Debbie Alli starts crying, so Harry puts his arm around him and then Vans Vertonghen says, 'Why not try the ladies? That's more in keeping with your general demeanours.'

So then Eric starts crying too, and Harry puts his arms around them and starts leading them out of the toilet. I turn to Toby and Vans, and ask them what their club's called. Vertonghen says, 'I bet you can't guess.' I say, 'Yodel.'

'How did you know that?'

I say, 'I just got lucky,' and I leave the toilets. I doubt it's the last I'll see of them, though...

ROBSON AND LAWRO GO FISHING

Mark Lawrenson has been trying to rebuild his life ever since the incident with the bear at Michael Owen's restaurant in Didsbury, but it's been the international break, which makes him happy because there's not much football on and he hates football.

He's been spending his spare time doing loads of things that he really likes – he's rewired his rabbit hutch (you know, those little wiry doors they have) – he's put a new one of them on, and he even sanded down and replaced the hinges on his neighbour's rabbit hutch. He spent a few days in his loft, re-plumping up his loft insulation; stared at a pigeon on next door's roof for a while; went outside and scraped all the shit out of the joints between the paving stones on the street outside his house – had a lovely time.

But the big event was... he went fishing with Robson Green. Not the EXTREME FISHING that Robson is famous for, where he catches sea cows and that. Just a nice day doing some quiet fishing on the river. Roach, trout, cod, a few tiddlers, that sort of thing.

They agreed that Robson would provide the fishing gear, and Mark said he'd bring along some bait. They stayed at a hotel near to the river the night before and, for dinner, Robson had two whole roast crabs and a bowl of ratatouille – he just ate the crabs with his hands and bit into them. Mark had a baked potato with tuna and sweetcorn – nice and simple.

They shared a room, which I thought was quite interesting. Mark didn't sleep very well because of Robson's snoring, so he spent most of the night sat up and just drawing on himself. He'd made a kind of homemade ink by mixing the coffee sachets in the room with a little bit of water. He found a tin of corned beef in Robson's bag and he snacked on that as well.

Next morning, they get to the river – Robson's all chirpy, as usual. 'Awwww, ah like yer shirt, Mark. It's nice and shiny and tight around your tits, like! So, what d'yer think the Toon's chances are this year under Rafa Benitez?'

But Mark says, 'I'm not really interested, Robson. I don't really like football. Can we just set up the rods?'

Robson ignores him and keeps banging on about Newcastle United. 'Aye, but havin' Rafa Benitez has got to be good. Ah mean, he's Rafa Benitez – he's lived abroad and talks daft and all that and everything I do, I do it for you...'

Mark just humours him, saying, 'Yeah, if you say so.'

Robson goes on: 'What d'yer reckon of Mike Ashley? D'yer reckon he's a bastard? Hey, is Mike Ashley a bastard?'

To which Mark says, 'I don't know, Robson. I've not met him – will you just set up my rod for me? I'm just nipping behind the bushes for a tod.'

So Robson sets up both the rods but then realises that he hasn't got the bait. He'd brought a tin of corned beef to use as bait, but it's gone. He shouts into the bushes at Mark, 'You know owt about this corned beef, soft lad?' – which, of course, he does, because he ate it in the middle of the night.

Mark confesses to having had the corned beef, and Robson says, 'Awww, man, yer fuckin' twat, like – how're we gonna fish now?'

Mark says, 'Don't worry, Robson – I've got an idea.'

So Mark goes behind the bushes and, when he comes back, in his open hand are fourteen niblets of corn that he's retrieved from his tod mound. Remember he had that tuna-and-sweetcorn baked potato the night before? Pretty resourceful, and he's even cut out little fishy shapes from his shiny silver suit to use as spinners for the bait.

Anyway, between them they caught six chub and four carp – the only downside was that Robson got food poisoning from handling Mark's corn niblets after he'd retrieved them from his tod.

It was nice for Mark, though, because he could have been the villain of the story but he turned it around and had a little victory, and that was just what he needed after the pest disaster with the bear at Michael Owen's ISIS restaurant.

WHO'S THE GREATEST – RONALDO OR MESSI?

We are arguably living through the greatest era for footballing talent, with two star players slugging it out in La Liga for the crown of 'Greatest Player of All Time'. But is leathery sex forward Cristiano Ronaldo the world's finest, or does the title belong to hamster-faced skill merchant Messi? Let's settle it once and for all as we pit them against each other in a series of key categories.

DIY SKILLS
With their bags of riches, neither player has ever felt the need to reach for their tools and knock up some CD shelves or sand down an old set of drawers before adding a fresh coat of varnish, or even white paint. Perhaps they're fearful of dropping a hammer on their precious feet, or perhaps they're just bone-idle.

RONALDO 0/10
MESSI 0/10

SNAKE CHARMING
Ronaldo was photographed near a snake on one occasion in 2005, although there is no concrete evidence to suggest that he charmed it out of a basket with a little flute first. As for Messi, he was raised in the slums of Argentina, where snake charming doesn't feature highly in a young boy's education – cattle rearing and warmongering are deemed to be more important instead. Both score poorly here and it's still neck and neck.

RONALDO: 0/10
MESSI 0/10

SUPERHERO POWERS

The competition is hotting up and there's not much between them here. Rumours persist that Messi once levitated himself in the first-class lounge at Barcelona Airport, while speculation that Ronaldo owns a cape refuses to go away.

RONALDO 2/10
MESSI 2/10

FOOTBALL SKILLS

Both players are really good at football. Hard to fault them.

RONALDO 8/10
MESSI 8/10

ADVERTISING SCOOTERS

The Argentine international triumphs hard in this category, thanks to his long-standing association with the £149.99 Messi Space Scooter. Perhaps fearful of copycat accusations, Ronaldo has stayed well away from the arena of scooter endorsement and is yet to get off the mark in this category, although there's still time to rectify that before he retires.

RONALDO 0/10
MESSI 10/10

FINAL SCORE
RONALDO 10/50
MESSI 20/50

THE WINNER: It's Lionel Messi!

AN AIRBORNE KISSING MIX-UP

I've just come back from the United States of America – I went to Palm Springs, visiting breweries, because I'm going to become a brewer. But that's another story for another time.

I flew first class, where you get your own bed and that, and I'll tell you who was on there with me – Simon Pegg from *Star Treks*, a chap called Biffy Clyro (who's a rock star), Mike out of Mike & The Mechanics. Mike wasn't with the rest of the Mechanics – I think they were in standard class, but he was with three women who were all identical to look at but different ages, but you'd only know if you cut into them to count the rings. Like Russian dolls, but then again not really. More like a tree. But I digress.

So I thought, 'Fuck me, I need to get myself involved with these three,' so I hung around with Simon Pegg for a bit, and he was watching a film about a kid who had special powers. Anyway, here's a bit of airline gossip for you – he declined to have the in-flight meal.

Biffy stood up for most of the flight, just drawing on himself with a marker pen, and Mike from Mike & The Mechanics went to the toilet three times, but his stride pattern and speed of approach to the toilet was identical every single time. Isn't that something?

That's the mark of a man who's travelled first class a LOT of times and is confident and extremely comfortable with the entire procedure. He knows who he is, he knows what he is and he knows where he's going and why he's going there. On three occasions, the toilet. Obviously, I can't be sure but I reckon he'll have delivered exactly the same volume every time: 33 cl, something like that.

Anyway, I'm in my bed cubicle, with the wife on one side beside me and some bloke in the bed on the other side. The stewardess was nice – big lass, quite masculine, with her hair in a bun and big, thick specs on. A bit retro, but I digress.

I don't know if you know this but, in first class, you have a big screen that you can pull out. I'm watching the movie that Simon Pegg had recommended about this kid with special powers and, suddenly, a box comes up on the screen and it goes 'PING'. The message says, 'Hello – you've been invited to live chat. Would you like to chat with the person in seat 11A?' So I just assume it's the wife, obviously – I have to respond, so I reply with, 'Yes, seat 10A would like to have a chat with you.' Then I put, 'Hello, 10A here again. Have you seen Mike from Mike & The Mechanics? He's on his way to the bogs again.' You know, just for a bit of fun – amuse the wife.

So the next message comes in response to that and it says, 'Do you fancy a kiss?' and I don't just get up and snog the wife – I type back in, 'Ooooh, you cheeky cheeky!' I climb up over the little divide between the two bed-cubicle things to approach the wife, and she's fast asleep.

It turns out it hasn't been her that I'm talking to – it was then that I realised that she was actually in seat 9A and not 11A. As I sit back down, the bloke next to me on the other side pops his head over his little barrier and he says, 'I'm waiting for my kiss...'

You think it's the Alderman, don't you? It's not – it's the fucking Town Clerk.

I couldn't believe it. I said, 'What are you doing on this flight?' Not angry, I wasn't angry, I was just a bit shocked – and, I'll admit, a little bit excited.

He says, 'I'll tell you what I'm doing – I'm waiting for my kiss.' So I think, fucking hell – I'll just get a little peck in and keep him happy. I quite fancied it anyway – I mean, the Town Clerk's a good-looking fella. Nice smooth skin, very photogenic, definitely worth a kiss.

Just as I lean in towards him, there's a little bit of turbulence and I hear the Tannoy go 'BEEEP BOOOP', and this voice goes, 'ROBERT! SIT DOWN! HOW DARE YOU PREPARE TO KISS MID-FLIGHT DURING TURBULENCE!'

I look up and there's the stewardess. She takes her wig off, and it's only the fucking Alderman! Turns out he's there with a load of kids in economy, and they all appear at the entrance curtain of the first-class bit, and they're all going, 'Kiss the Alderman! Kiss the Alderman!' Him and the Town Clerk are taking a load of daft kids – you know, kids without much of a future. They're taking a load of dreary kids over to Universal, or whatever the fuck it's called, in Los Angeles.

So they're all chanting, 'Kiss the Alderman! Kiss the Alderman!' so I lean in again. Just then, the wife pops up! 'ROBERT! WHAT IS GOING ON, ROBERT? DURING THIS FLIGHT, ROBERT!' And there's nothing I can say. What can I say? That I'm about to kiss the Alderman?

The Alderman scurries off and he sits next to Biffy and starts drawing on Biffy's face for him. He spent the rest of the flight with Biffy, actually. I was a bit jealous – they were having a right laugh.

Another failed kiss incident with the Alderman, and it's getting a bit complicated now that the Town Clerk's getting involved.

A HISTORY
OF FOOTBALL

PART THREE
THE EIGHTIES

March 1980: Jack Watts and Keith Mullin – joint owners of Southend United – formally dissolve their partnership in court, but both retain control of the club, deciding to share custody on alternate weekends. If a match is postponed, whoever has custody will have to take 15,000 Southend fans swimming, followed by a kickabout in the park and some ice cream on the sea front.

September 1980: FIFA conclude their experiment with the abolition of gravity, which has taken place over the past nine months in the Swedish Ninth Division. Players wore helmets lined with lead in order to deal with the removal of the gravitational force, and attendances soared. However, the trial was deemed a failure afterwards, as over four hundred items of jewellery were lost by players and never retrieved. FIFA's next experimental rule change will see players in Botswana's League of Indomitable Challengers taking to the field sporting the fashions of 1964.

October 1980: Eyebrows are raised after Brian Clough dumps Ian Wallace outside the City Ground for five hours. The popular Nottingham Forest striker is tied to a lamp post, naked and covered in strips of raw meat that were glued to his body. The stunt is believed to be in a bid to set up a swap deal with Ipswich Town's Alan Brazil in the forthcoming transfer window. Clough does not deny his part in the incident, but is quoted as saying, 'Why have transfers got anything to do with it?'

May 1981: Controversial referee Martin Debenham retires. Nicknamed 'Dracula' for his habit of refereeing in a black cape and for biting the necks of players as he was sending them off, Debenham was wheeled on to the Wembley turf in a coffin before the 1976 FA Cup Final. After retirement, he relocates to Transylvania and becomes a property developer.

April 1982: Veteran non-league midfielder Martin Hoskins' lifelong ambition is finally realised when his club, Cherringham Swallows, graciously allows him to become chairman for a day. Hoskins, by day a sausage technician, says, 'I've turned out for the Cherubs for twenty-three years now, and I have to thank the chairman, Frank Wiskey, for giving me the chance to sit in the hot seat, albeit just for a day.'

During his twenty-four-hour tenure, Hoskins awards himself a highly paid professional contract with a backdated salary stretching back to 1959, hands out lifelong bans to all season-ticket holders in the Peel Street end, who he says have had a running grudge against him, sells the club's ground to a local property developer, who also happens to be his brother-in-law, and agrees a merger with local rivals Ferringham Daggers.

Hoskins later says, 'It was an eye-opening experience and, now that I realise how much hard work goes on behind the scenes, I'm glad I'm just a humble player.'

May 1982: In an attempt to eradicate unnecessary pre-tournament injuries, the Spanish FA decides to wrap the World Cup squad in cotton wool until the start of the tournament. Each player is inserted into a giant, individually moulded blue egg, which is then been placed inside a man-sized matchbox padded with sheets of cotton wool. Each matchbox is labelled with the player's name and stored in the basement of the team hotel in Madrid.

Says manager José Santamaría, 'We will be hatching each egg just before our first game against Switzerland.'

June 1982: Speedy Aberdeen winger Mark Nesmith reveals the secret behind his lightning pace during an interview with *Shoot*. He says that he imagines he is being chased by a giant, bald ghost that wants to touch his arse.

September 1982: Under-fire Peterborough boss Alan Judd breaks the club's transfer record, spending £15,000 on a giant bouncy castle. He says, 'I know it's not strictly a footballer, but we can put it in the car park on hot days and the kids will love it.' Judd is sacked later that week and is believed to have had a nervous breakdown after his wife leaves him for a man named Peter Borough.

January 1983: Bradford defender John Woodstone becomes the first player to openly admit he is suffering from a penis injury. He says, 'The game is flooded with injuries to the penis, but they continually get pushed aside into the groin category. I'm not ashamed to stand up and say I've hurt my cock, and maybe I can go some way to removing the stigma.' As a result of his comments, Woodstone has been thrown out of the PFA and his club claim never to have heard of him.

July 1983: Howard Wilkinson plans to steal a march on his rivals next season by forcing his Sheffield Wednesday players to train wearing bodysuits made of silver foil. Wilkinson says, 'I love Corn Flakes, me, and I noticed they'd started putting them in silver foil bags to keep them fresher. I could tell the difference as soon as I bit into some, and I thought, 'Aye-aye, Howard, think on because there's some kind of a plan to be hatched here.' Each player receives one foil suit on 2 July and is forbidden to remove it until shortly before the kick-off of the first match of the season six weeks later.

September 1983: The long-standing tradition of halting a match just before the end so that players and fans can sing 'Happy Birthday' to any player who is celebrating his special day comes to an end. The last player to be sung to is Wimbledon's Nigel Winterburn, and the old birthday cake and candles that were scrapped are revived as a one-off to mark the occasion.

The cake was withdrawn from the on-pitch birthday

celebrations in 1974, along with the bumps, and, following the change to the rules in 1983, players can only sing 'Happy Birthday' to a team-mate if they do it really quickly, in the first example of what becomes the pre-match huddle.

October 1983: Middlesbrough have a request to postpone their match with Bristol Rovers turned down by the FA after their excuse of 'We turned up this morning and there were thousands of horses on the pitch' isn't deemed worthy of postponement.

January 1984: East Fife shock the footballing world by signing a cartoon character, Jason from the hit kids' show *Battle of the Planets*. Cynics write off the deal as a desperate attempt to gain publicity, and Jason only makes four substitute appearances for the club. He leaves the club at the end of the season after a video appears showing him in a three-in-a-bed session with Smurfette and The New Shmoo.

June 1984: Mexican legend Hugo Arujo finally retires from the game at the age of forty-eight, having been a first team regular with CF Monterrey since he was just nine years of age. The club offer to retire his Number 11 shirt, but Arujo goes further and asks to be cemented into the exterior of the club's stadium for ever more, wearing his strip and covered by a tarpaulin sheet to keep the rain off. Fans make the pilgrimage to visit Arujo every day, bringing him food and drink, and reading Agatha Christie novels to him, which are a particular favourite of the tricky winger.

October 1984: Liverpool midfielder Jan Mølby decides not to play in the crunch match against Chelsea, as the game coincides with the sacred Finnish festival of Ticklemas. It occurs on the one day of the year when it stays dark for twenty-four hours and everyone takes off their clothes, drinks vodka and tickles each other for the entire day.

Mølby eventually plays in the match after Joe Fagan intercepts him at Liverpool Airport, reminding him that he is from Denmark and not Finland and, therefore, has no right to go to Ticklemas.

November 1984: Fans of North-East minnows West Auckland Town, and romantic football fans everywhere, are in deep shock after new evidence shows that the club didn't actually win the World Cup in 1909 and 1911, as widely believed. The grandson of former club historian Bob Gosling has found a written confession from his long-dead grandfather stating that the whole thing was a hoax and was, in fact, only a boast that he had dreamed up in order to procure sex from gullible women in the town.

March 1985: Two Burton Albion players celebrate after discovering that they are actually long-lost twin brothers. Strike partners Tim and Tom Shepton have played for the club for three years, scoring 165 goals in just 109 games, but always assumed their mutual understanding on the pitch, uncanny similarity and shared birthdays were just a spooky coincidence. Tim said, 'It all came out in the open when the rest of the lads were comparing their birth certificates after training one day.' Tom and I didn't have ours and, when we asked our mums about it, it turned out they were the same woman. It's amazing.'

Mrs Shepton later faces seven charges of bigamy.

August 1985: Supporters are banned from carrying electric guitars into Football League matches following a controversial new ruling. Electric guitar users claim they're being discriminated against, as the rules still allow acoustic and bass guitars to be wielded on the terraces.

March 1986: Oxford United midfielder Steve Peacock starts wearing blinkers during matches, as he finds himself becoming increasingly distracted by pitch-side advertising. The Welsh Under-21 international says, 'The ads are really well made these days, by skilled, creative professionals. They're so alluring that I often find myself giving the ball away cheaply as I ponder whether or not to switch to a high-interest-rate current account.' Peacock's manager announces that the player will be released at the end of his contract in the summer.

August 1986: With attendances at their worst for thirty-five years, Macclesfield Town come up with an ingenious plan to create football's first 'drive thru' stadium. Chairman Barry Gibb says, 'We reduced the size of the pitch so that cars could drive round it. We charged a pound a pop and, for another pound, the reserves would wash your car on the way out. It worked very well for the first two weeks – attendances were up fifty per cent – but we had to stop it when one customer lost control and mowed down our right-back.'

October 1986: Leicester's recent 1-1 draw with Cardiff has hidden meanings if played backwards, claims a leading occultist and video-cassette ruiner. Dermot Boon says, 'I've watched it backwards three times now and, each time, Alan Smith has ordered me to burn down a local pub during his post-match interview at the start, which, of course, I have done. Fortunately, I don't drink, though.' A spokesman for Boon's local brewery said, 'There's a reason why football matches aren't usually played backwards and we're certain that this is it. Our drinkers are finding it most inconvenient.'

February 1987: Ipswich Town midfielder Lance Mannion announces his retirement from the game due to his religious beliefs. He says that God has told him that he must only pick the ball up with his hands and carry it into the goal from now on – something which the referee, crowd and other players disagree with during Town's FA Cup tie against Hereford United.

August 1987: Carlisle United bosses are criticised after trying something a bit different for their half-time entertainment during a home FA Cup tie against Barnet. A cash-prize game in which opposing fans raced to smash an erotic ice sculpture in the quickest time for £25 is regarded by some as unsuitable for a family football match, mainly due to the fans' nudity.

September 1987: The latest plan to foil hooliganism is launched, with fans searched at the turnstiles and stripped of their nicknames, courtesy of a new law stating that they have to use their full forenames at all times when referring to each other. Minister for Sport, Colin Moynihan, says, 'The chances of someone being whipped up into a violent frenzy when being referred to by his peers as "Tarquin" or "Tristram", rather than "Knacker", are reduced considerably with the introduction of this law.'

November 1987: Paul Corner makes his Southampton debut aged just fifteen years and eleven days, and is described as 'a cross between Maradona and Little Jimmy Osmond.' Sadly, though, it all goes wrong for Corner – he makes just six first-team appearances, and is last heard of working in a paint factory, drinking gloss to test it for poison.

January 1988: Alloa Athletic scrap their controversial decision to allow fans to give birth on the pitch after a difficult and prolonged labour interferes with their recent basement battle with Arbroath. Supporter Mary Langley finally delivers 8lb 6oz son Frankie in the seventy-seventh minute of the match beneath a protective sheet of tarpaulin as the match goes on around her. Club secretary Maurice Hobbs says, 'We've had people married and ashes scattered on the pitch, so we thought we'd try for the hat trick, but never again. Ross Hamilton slipped on the afterbirth and did his hamstring, putting him out for a month. It's not worth it.'

November 1988: Tranmere midfielder and long-throw specialist Steve Weaton voluntarily has some of the tendons in his arms removed after he becomes too good at throw-ins.

Weaton's throws have become so powerful that they either sail straight across the pitch and out of the ground or thud into the faces of helpless fans in Row Z. Sadly, the op goes wrong, his arms are severely weakened, and he is forced to quit the game. The club take pity on him and give him a job for life carrying the physio's magic sponge, which is as much as he is able to lift.

May 1989: After the Third Division play-off final, losing Oxford United manager Steve Briggs makes off with the golden ticket to Division Two, which was supposed to be presented to victorious Wigan Athletic. Briggs then disappears and is not seen again throughout the summer months – a situation that leads Oxford to appoint a new manager in his place. He finally makes a reappearance on the opening day of the following season as Wigan prepare to play their first Division Two match at Doncaster. Briggs brandishes the golden ticket and insists that he is allowed to take on Doncaster himself. He is quickly tranquillised and jailed.

June 1989: FIFA finally takes action following the epidemic of ghost players that has swept through the game in recent months, with all spectres now banned from the field of play. The first one to appear during a match was Boca Juniors legend Hector Rodriguez, who died in 1974 but whose ghost appeared during the Argentine Cup Final seven years later, popping up to head the winner – ironically, after carrying his head under his arm for most of the match. The floodgates then opened and scores of ghosts were summoned by desperate clubs looking to gain an advantage by recruiting spooky stars. After the FIFA ban, the ghosts go on to form the breakaway Dead Legends tournament, which is still played every summer.

September 1989: Controversial referee Roger Piper retires – he became notorious for blowing for full-time just as teams were about to take decisive penalty kicks, sometimes as early as twenty minutes before the end of the match. Piper still holds the world record for the most death threats received in a single season (4,837).

THE SECRET SOCCER SUPERSTAR'S MYSTERY PLAYERS

Greetings. I am the Secret Soccer Superstar and I have played football at the highest level for many clubs. Seriously, I'm not lying. I know so many secrets about top, top players and managers that, if I didn't share a few of them in the public domain, I would probably have some kind of brain spasm.

So here are some red-hot secrets about some of the biggest names in the game. Can you guess who they are? The answers are obvious to me because I am the Secret Soccer Superstar, but they certainly won't be to you...

Who are the players who, for £100,000 each, agreed to take part in a life-size table-football match, with iron bars strapped across their backs? The game took place in the garden of the grinning head of a Far Eastern gambling syndicate.

Which former international defender pays the BBC to produce an alternative version of *The Archers* featuring personalised plot lines developed by himself and his wife?

Who is the pacy striker who has paid £500,000 for a

mocked-up holographic film of himself and Barack Obama white-water rafting down the Niagara Falls?

Who is the veteran midfielder who has bought 1980s chart stars Hue & Cry and has them playing live in his home gym for seventeen hours a day?

Which EPL megastar has built a pine holiday home on top of a pole 150ft above the ground so that he can declare it an independent state and charge his children a 60 per cent 'Super Tax'?

Which under-fire manager has taken to whispering his team talks into his assistant's ear before sitting back and watching as the hapless sidekick then relays the instructions to the team via the medium of mime?

Which unfunny TV pundit bought the 'tactics truck' from ITV's ill-fated *The Premiership* show, and has adapted it into a mobile disco, which he hires out for the secret woodland satanic rituals that are *de rigueur* among the game's top earners?

Who is the foreign import who is actually a hermaphrodite and blames his complicated genital arrangement on a child-hood experiment with hydrochloric acid?

Who is the Premier League chairman who canvassed for a place on the FA executive committee by sending out mocked-up pictures of his head attached to the body of Beyoncé Knowles?

Who is the on-loan international defender who has started a bitter smear campaign against a local menswear shop, handing out leaflets accusing them of sub-standard stitching?

Which Premier League manager insisted on watching an

international midfielder sign for his club through a two-way mirror while his chairman spanked him with a bass guitar?

Which veteran League One manager has a doppelganger who stands in for him for six months of the year while the real manager spends the time in the Virgin Islands with his face wrapped in bandages?

Who is the veteran goalkeeper who intends to play until he's sixty-five thanks to his regular intake of liquidised telephone directories, which he believes contain anti-ageing qualities?

Who is the former Premier League chairman who is trying to raise the funds for a return to the game by providing cheap back-street dental treatments?

Which outspoken midfielder is angling for a transfer to a rival club in order to be nearer to two of his three wives?

Which club has threatened to take the FA to court in order to get their wish of playing in flesh-coloured body stockings granted?

Who is the London-based international full-back who won't play without his pet frog cradled under his shirt in a sling?

Which cultured veteran full-back collects the skulls of the chimps from the PG Tips adverts?

Who is the tricky winger who owns 33 per cent of a company that aims to pioneer the inflatable shagpile carpet?

Which midfield hard-man likes to build giant papier-mâché statues in his garden with widescreen televisions for eyes?

Which prolific striker stays fresh during the summer months by travelling to the Swiss Alps, where alternative gurus catapult him into the side of snow-covered mountains?

Who is the eccentric international who enjoys an unusual type of acupuncture by sleeping for two hours each afternoon on a cactus?

Who is the Championship manager who can't sleep without the sound of World War Two air raid sirens playing in the background?

Which goalkeeper accidentally crushed his only winner's medal in his kitchen sink waste-disposal unit while he was pissed?

Which relegation-threatened squad spent the whole of last week team bonding by staging a performance of *Starlight Express*?

Who is the combative midfielder who likes to relax inside a block of ice wearing nothing but shorts and licking a blue handgun?

Which Scottish international was spotted trying to give away some old reggae seven-inch singles outside a retirement home?

Which injured striker spends his days cold-calling thousands of homeowners, offering them insurance against brain injuries caused by toxic tinsel?

CASPER, I LOVE YOU (PART ONE)

Sad story, this one. It's been a difficult week for Steve McClaren. For about a year now, he's had a problem with his shoulder – maybe a torn tendon, something like that. It's made it very difficult for him to carry Casper, his yellow snake, around his neck like he likes to.

Steve decides to go to the doctor to get the shoulder looked at. The doctor says, 'Take your top off,' and, when he does, there's a sort of acne-type poxy rash on his shoulder. The doctor starts examining it then starts poking at it with a teaspoon. Then he just prises the whole lot off Steve's shoulder: it's a layer of dried snake sick; an accumulation that's gone crispy on his skin.

They both laugh. Steve says, 'Bloody Casper – he's been dribbling on my shoulder when I've had him wrapped around my neck,' and the doctor laughs, but adds that it obviously isn't the cause of Steve's shoulder problem. It's probably something internal, like a tendon.

As he's getting his blood pressure done, Steve starts explaining that he's out of a job at the moment, that Casper's not been very well and that the Fat Lass is starting to get really nasty because Steve's around the house so much these days. He says that she's even threatened to make him choose between her and the snake. She's had enough of the snake spew – it's getting in her haversack, her DM's, her fleeces and her leggings, and she's at the end of her tether with all of it.

As an aside, did you know that Steve spent almost £1,000 on a pair of purple satin Jimmy Choob shoes to try to keep her off his back? She usually wears DM's when she's down the social club and that but, when there's a wedding or something, she puts her Jimmy Choobs on. She can't really walk in them, but you know...

The doctor realises that Steve's depressed, so he gives him some happy pills. Tells him not to take them on an empty stomach – take them with a glass of milk. Steve lobs a couple of them down there and then, and he's as happy as Larry within an hour.

He's at home, watching the cartoons and singing his favourite song, 'Convoy'. *I got a brand new convoy / Travelling through the night / Look out 'cos here's my convoy / All the other convoys are shite...'*

He even goes into the garage and starts up his clown car, just to keep it ticking over – which he hasn't done in ages because he's been feeling so low. In spite of all this, the one thing that's still getting him down is Casper, because the snake hasn't been well and is really down in the dumps. The other day, Steve even caught Casper chewing at one of his own tods – awful.

With hindsight, this was pretty daft but Steve thinks that, maybe if he gives Casper one of his happy pills, the snake might soon be feeling as good as Steve is. So he crushes one of the pills up and puts it inside a mouse for Casper, to see if it'll help cheer him up.

The pill kicks in pretty quick and Casper starts dancing on the kitchen floor, spiralling and zig-zagging across the black-and-white tiles. He's bouncing off the kitchen units, making an 'S'-shape and that.

Unfortunately for Casper, the Fat Lass is trying to cook a big pot of beans at the same time and he bangs right into her legs. She turns around and she can see him darting about – a flash of colour on the black-and-white checked tiles of the kitchen floor. She starts feeling a bit nauseous and starts realising that she's about to go into a fit because of all the strobing with Casper bouncing around. Kitchen strobing's the worst of the lot.

She can't look away and she's heading for a fit, so she boots Casper full force, hard as she can – he goes straight in the air, he ricochets off the kitchen island, smashes into the venetian blinds on the window, then he just drops down like a sack of tod. Lifeless.

To be continued…

GANGS OF THE EPL – THE RETURN OF THE SPURS GANG

So I went to a charity do in London – of course, with it being in London, it was to raise money to save a daft building that's being turned into a newer, dafter building. All of London's 'glitterati' were there – Shane Richie, Liz Cundy, Natalie Cassidy, Bruno Tonioli, Len Goodman, Fleur West? East? West? East? East. And Alex Reid, the cross-dressing cage fighter who used to live in Jordan. It was a quality do – a proper sit-down for dinner – so, obviously, it was lamb shanks for most of the courses.

But the time came when I needed to go to the toilet, of course. I walk in there and it's empty, apart from Harry Kane and Eric Dier, the Tottenham lads. I feel like I'm being ambushed. I can sense that they're waiting for me, in their tight black thin polo necks, tight black skinny trousers and pointy black shoes, black gloves, and big white pendants around their necks in the shape of hearts.

Straight away, Harry Kane says, 'We've been waiting for you, baldy. You've made a big mistake coming here – you gave away the name of our secret club last week and we are furious, to say the least!'

Eric Dier chirps in, 'Yes, we had to change our secret-club name, which is very inconvenient. Key rings, membership cards, club wallets, the list just bloody goes on and on. But you'll never guess the new name, unless you have special skills like Darren Brown or Ali Bongo, and we doubt very much that you do have those skills.'

I shouldn't have really, but I said, 'Is it The White Harts?' – you know, 'cos of the pendants. At that moment, Debbie

Alli BANGS his way out of one of the cubicles. 'Awwww, fucking hell! He knows the secret name – did one of you tell him?' So Harry says, 'No, it turns out he's got special powers like Darren Brown – what rotten luck for us.'

They all looked really sad so I said, 'Honestly, look, your secret's safe with me – I'm not interested in your club. But what do you get up to?' Eric said, 'Don't answer him: it's a trap. He's fishing for an exclusive story on our club.'

Then Debbie chips in, really cocky, like – 'That rings true with me, so he can tell everyone how we draw pictures of cars and swap YouTube clips of tit models.'

'Awww, fucking hell, Debbie,' says Harry Kane. 'Now he knows everything – you have given him the ammunition to bring this club to its bloody knees.' Debbie, 'cos he's been told off by Harry, storms out of the toilets.

So I said, 'Obviously, you've ambushed me – what did you intend to do with me?' Harry says, 'We were going to give you a right telling-off.' Eric says, 'We even discussed splashing you with water that's not fresh.' But then – and it's technically right – Harry says, 'We can't do anything now, 'cos we're not quorate!' It's technically right, because Debbie's gone.

BANG! Another cubicle opens – out comes Toby Alderweireld and Vans Vertonghen in the green suits with Robin Hood hats on. Toby starts slowly clapping his hands – 'Bravo. Bravo, Mister Robert Mortimer. You are most efficient.'

'Yes,' says Vans. 'And you have saved us the job of discovering the name of these fools' secret club. They will have to get new branding! Yes, that means new key rings, mugs, membership cards, the whole caboodle.'

Anyway, so Harry Kane says, 'Come on, we're getting out of here – there's a bad smell in here.'

'That will be the shit I've just had,' says David Seaman, who's just come out of the far cubicle.

So I'm left with Toby and Vans. Toby says, 'You will never discover the name of our secret club, unless you have a machine like the one that broke the Enigma code or equivalent technology.' I say, 'Is it The Merry Men?' – 'cos they've got the Robin Hood hats on.

'Ha, ha, ha, ha!' says Vans. 'No.'

I said, 'Is it The Hood Club?'

'Ha, ha, ha – no, you weak sausage!'

So I said, 'Is it The Sherwood Club?' Fucking hell – Toby's lips begin to quiver, and Vans comes over to me and starts patting me down.

'Where is your machine? Where is it? Who are you working for? Is it Theo Walcott's gang? Tell me or we will throw damp hand towels at you!'

So I thought I'd be a naughty, and I said, 'Awww, please don't do that, Vans, I beg of you. Yes, I admit it – I'm working for Theo's gang.'

'We knew it. We knew it! Come on, Toby, we will have to tell Harry about this. We need to join forces and take on Theo as a powerful unit!'

And that was just the start of it…

ROBSON AND LAWRO'S EXTREME BANGERS

Robson Green and Mark Lawrenson had a fishing trip together a couple of weeks ago and, when Mark got home, he was really excited and he said to his wife, 'Alright, Barbara?'

She said, 'Had a nice day with Robson Green off the telly?' and he handed her one of his Belinda Wipes – they're one of these special wipes that he favours. They come in a big roll, like a kitchen roll, and they've got air pockets for extra absorption. You can mainly only get them in decorators' outlets, not in supermarkets. Industrial strength.

So anyway, she wipes his face for him with a Belinda Wipe, because he's so excited that he's gone a bit clammy, and Mark says, 'Yeah, I'm going to ask Robson if he'll be my friend.' Barbara says, 'That's a good idea, Mark. Why don't you give him a ring now?' to which he breathlessly replies, 'Oh, I will!'

Mark goes off and phones up Robson, and says to him, 'Hi, Robson. I enjoyed fishing with you – would you like to be my friend?' Robson, who hasn't got all that many friends on account of him being a bit too chirpy, is cock-a-hoop at this.

'Awwww, I'd love it if ah became yer friend, ah'd absolutely love it, like. Maybe you could arrange for us to meet Rafa Benitez – eh, yer could arrange that for me, couldn't yer, eh, like?'

Mark says, 'Ah, I don't know about that…'

'Hey! Ah know!' shouts Robson. 'I'm doing me EXTREME

SAUSAGE stall at Penrith market tomorra – would yer like to help us oot?'

'Yes, I'd love to,' replies Mark. 'That sounds very wholesome. Would you mind if I tried to flog some of my hairspray range? I've got about a hundred canisters left to flog.'

Robson's fine with this, saying, 'Aww, no problem, like – here, you never know, Rafa Benitez might be there. Ah know foreigners like markets, like.'

Mark is cautious, saying, 'Well I don't know about that.'

Next day, Mark arrives at Robson's stall in his Hyundai and is greeted with, 'Alreeet, Lawro? You haven't brought Rafa with yer, have yer? Only jokin'!'

Mark says, 'Look, Robson, can we not talk about Rafa, please. I don't like football.'

Anyway, Robson fires up his grill and starts cooking his EXTREME BANGERS. He calls them that because he does a show called *Extreme Fishing*, where he catches big eels and river cows and stuff like that, so these are big, EXTREME BANGERS.

Mark arranges his hairspray on the display and it's not long before business is pretty brisk. Then, in a bit of a lull, Mark announces that he's going to wipe down the grill with his Belinda Wipes, so he turns off the gas and starts to clean it.

Suddenly. there's a bit of a commotion in the market, and word spreads that… listen up… Rafa Benitez has turned up! At Penrith market! Robson's cock is now a total hoop. Three hundred and sixty degrees. He shouts, 'Quick! Fire up the grill! Rafa's here! He might want one of me extreme porkers! Come on, Mark, hurry up!'

Mark's a bit flummoxed, but he gets the gas back on and fires it up. Unfortunately, he's left a load of his Belinda Wipes on the grill and they catch fire. The whole roll of them catches fire, so he sort of flicks at it with a fish slice until it rolls off. The only problem is it lands in among the hairspray. 'Fucking hell!' says Mark.

Next thing, Rafa appears on the scene. Robson yells, 'Here comes Rafa! He's coming over to the stall! I canna believe it!'

Then… BANG! A hairspray canister explodes. 'Fuck me!' says Mark.

Obviously, Rafa's security immediately think it's ISIS, so one of them runs over, punches Robson in his tits, and another drags Rafa away at great speed. 'Ahhh, shit, man!' bawls Robson.

Mark gets the fire extinguisher out of his Hyundai and puts out the flames, while Robson is shouting after the Newcastle manager, 'Rafa! Rafa! Come back and have a sausage! Have a monster porker!' But it's too late – Rafa's gone, so Mark puts his arm around Robson and says, 'Never mind – I'll arrange for you to meet him because you're my best friend.'

And then he says, 'Hey, Robson – now THAT'S what I call an extreme banger!' and they both laugh until they stop laughing.

FOOTBALLERS IN THE WILD (PART THREE)

Here's another batch of our favourite player sightings from the Footballers in the Wild section of the Athletico Mince podcast.

ÀNGEL RANGEL on the balcony of some riverside flats, trying to see how easy it is to chuck a shopping trolley into the water.

JESSE LINGARD at a self-service checkout up the Asda, buying four pairs of flip-flops and some glue.

JOE ALLEN in the back of a cab, carrying a massive fish in a carrier bag, on the phone to someone, going on and on about how big his bath is.

RAFAEL VAN DER VAART at Liverpool coach station, drinking milk and swearing.

DIDIER DROGBA in a posh shop in Milan, wearing a false moustache and carrying a poodle under his arm.

SAIDO BERAHINO wandering around Birmingham city centre, wearing a muscle vest and shouting 'Big boy coming through' out of a megaphone.

LEE CATTERMOLE outside St James' Park, muttering to himself before trying to shoulder-charge the Leazes End.

ANDY CARROLL hitchhiking by the side of the road on the outskirts of Portsmouth. He was holding a piece of cardboard with 'Glory' scribbled on it.

STEVEN GERRARD in a chip shop in Bolton. When a customer asked him for an autograph, he denied being Gerrard, claiming he was a plumber called Len Benson and he was only there to check the drains.

PAUL POGBA on the teacups at Legoland, wearing a Wigan Athletic shirt.

BRYAN ROBSON sat in the back of taxi in London, doodling on a notepad. He left it behind when he got out and he'd done a picture of Midge Ure buried up to his neck in porridge.

Three CRISTIANO RONALDO lookalikes (or triplets) outside Old Trafford, carrying football boots and crying.

MOHAMED ELMOHAMADY hanging around in the car park at Hull City, offering to do face-painting for passers-by.

JOE LEDLEY standing outside Coral and wearing a Crystal Palace scarf as a nappy.

JORDAN IBE collecting a cape from a Bournemouth dry-cleaners.

OLIVIER GIROUD at Islington Town Hall, roaring, 'But why do I have to pay council tax if I'm invisible?'

JASON PUNCHEON stuck in a lift, thinking he could get the doors open by tickling them. He was wrong.

TOM CLEVERLEY in Costa, wearing a long hippy wig.

JURGEN KLOPP bartering over a sheepskin rug in a shop. It was for sale at £75; Klopp was offering £7.99.

BASTIAN SCHWEINSTIGER dancing in front of some traffic lights in Edinburgh at 5am.

EMMANUEL ADEBAYOR queuing outside Glastonbury in February, saying he wanted to be first in so he could get down the front.

DUŠAN TADIĆ doing 'Space Oddity' on the karaoke in The Grey Horse in Southampton. At the end, he jumped off the speaker stack.

GORDON STRACHAN on the outskirts of Bolton, getting out of his car and throwing what looked like a fur-trapper's hat into a skip.

STEVEN FLETCHER in Ikea in Bolton, wearing a fur-trapper's hat and eating an ice lolly.

JUAN MATA coming out of a tattoo parlour with a fresh tartan dog on the side of his face.

JOHN TERRY coming out of the disabled toilets at Disneyland Paris.

SHOLA AMEOBI outside a stationery shop in Ipswich, where he'd bought half a tonne of Gloy.

JORDON MUTCH at a local dog rescue centre, carrying a magic wand and a blueberry muffin.

JOHN HARTSON in the neck injury department of Cardiff Hospital, boasting that Arsène Wenger wants him at Arsenal again for one last season.

PATRICK VIEIRA in B&M with a man dressed as a butler. They were arguing and pushing each other.

YAYA TOURE on the top deck of a bus, leafing through a catalogue of WAGs.

DARREN BENT driving up the A1(M) in a mobile home that had 'Beep Beep – It's The Dazza Van' painted on the side.

AIDEN McGEADY panic-buying petrol in Edinburgh. He was jumping up and down and squealing like a girl.

STEPEHEN IRELAND in the back of a cab, trying to pay the fare with some chocolate coins, and leaving a finger of Fudge as a tip.

KI SUNG-YEUNG taking a Jay-Z CD back to Tesco in Swansea, and complaining that there wasn't enough swearing in it.

MAARTEN STEKELENBURG at Chester Zoo, trying to find the orangutan that he's adopted but convinced that it works in the gift shop.

CRISTIANO RONALDO emerging from an old tin mine in Cornwall at 6am, telling a tramp that he'd been UFO-spotting.

JEFF SCHLUPP at a bus stop in Leicester, scrawling something on the bag of a fag packet and asking a child how to spell 'licence'.

NEYMAR in a petrol station in Aberdeen, buying £3.75 worth of diesel and a packet of Hubba Bubba, and trying to pay with a £500 note.

JACK GREALISH asleep in the back of a taxi, waking up and shouting, 'Put it in my hand, Mr Mandela!' before he realising where he was.

JASON PUNCHEON stuck in a lift for six hours, asking if he could eat his hair, as he was so hungry.

SHAUN WRIGHT-PHILLIPS arriving at Stansted Airport, carrying a crate of live chickens. He was getting them to sing by blowing a whistle in their faces.

TONY PULIS buying an *Indiana Jones* DVD box set in HMV, dressed up as the character and cracking his whip at a woman who might have been his mum.

JACK RODWELL in the back of a taxi, asking the cabbie to drive round and round for eight hours while he watched episodes of *Scooby Doo* on his iPad.

DARREN FLETCHER at a garden centre near Yeovil, possibly with Robert Mugabe.

PHIL NEVILLE in the back of a taxi, asking the driver to turn up 'Pump Up the Jam' when it came on.

ARJEN ROBBEN in a costume-hire shop, asking if they do a 'Johnny Clackers suit'.

MICHAEL LAUDRUP in Bristol city centre, buying a Russian translation book, and paying for it with one of those big charity cheques.

AARON CRESWELL in Wolverhampton, trying to eat a parking ticket that he'd just got.

TITUS BRAMBLE in the car park of a Wigan garden centre, handing out printed copies of his blog about the best garden centres in the Wigan area.

FRANK LAMPARD at an ice-cream van in Slough, asking for a Super Duper Tutti Frutti, 'like what they do in New York.' The bloke didn't sell them so he settled for a Screwball and a Mars Bar 'for later on.'

THE FOREIGN BILLIONAIRES WHO COULD SOON BE OWNING YOUR CLUB

No self-respecting football club is without an overseas billionaire owner these days – but there's a still a few monied foreigners who are yet to snap one up. Here are the ones who could soon be in charge at a club near you...

VLADIMIR LUBLIN: Russian billionaire. Lublin built his fortune after winning Russia's steel industry in a game of cards. He lists his hobbies as skiing, football and murdering business rivals. Lifelong Middlesbrough fan.

RAVASHING WAKANITRAMPONG: President for life of Vietnam. Wakanitrampong recently celebrated his sixty-seventh birthday by abolishing democracy and marrying one of his daughters. Linked with Birmingham City.

CROWN PRINCE BIN AL BIN RAK BIN MAN AL SAUD: Member of the Saudi Royal Family. Said to be interested in buying a Premier League club as a birthday surprise for his horrible son. Rumoured to have purchased Reading for his eldest daughter, who then swapped the Berkshire club for an iPod Touch.

ANDY NURK: American Internet billionaire and *Star Trek* fanatic. Thirty-three-year-old Nurk hopes that purchasing a football club will enable him to meet girls. He wants to take over Everton, reshape the stadium into a replica of the planet Vulcan and install the ghost of Leonard Nimoy as Director of Football.

A HISTORY
OF FOOTBALL

PART FOUR
THE NINETIES

May 1990: Vultures are circling over the clubs facing make-or-break relegation battles on the last day of the season – literally! Leading vulture supplier Tennysons arrange for ten of the birds to fly above stadiums housing clubs whose fates were still unknown going into the final fixture. In Scotland, where vultures are banned, their place is taken by turkeys.

November 1990: Carlisle United bosses are criticised after trying something a bit different for their half-time entertainment during a home FA Cup tie against Colchester United. The sight of former players, who had been supplied with free alcohol since noon, playing a charity five-a-side match is regarded by some as unsuitable for a family football match, mainly due to the nudity.

August 1991: Hard-up Peterborough United attempt to raise some much-needed cash by having their nickname sponsored on a month-to-month basis in the coming season. Throughout August, the team will be known as 'The WarmPussy Cat Sanctuaries' and, over the following months, their nicknames will include 'The Rudi Goombay – Kids Party Magicians' and 'The Hamer's Builders Sands – Two Tonnes For The Price Of One'.

October 1991: A massive manhunt is launched as rogue football agent Tony DuPrez goes missing after selling a dozen fictional players to lower-league clubs. DuPrez has shown videos of actual players to the clubs and agreed fees for the pretend stars, most of whom play for pretend clubs, pocketing over £2 million for himself. He is finally found living in a hedge in Gateshead, and it is discovered that the cash has disappeared after he paid it into a pretend bank account.

January 1992: Arsenal's Tony Adams is sent off for swallowing the ball during a league game against Leeds United. A direct free kick from Gary McAllister heads straight into the Arsenal wall and Adams opens his giant mouth, swallowing the ball with a single gulp.

March 1992: Highly rated youngster Robbie Moffatt makes his debut for Burnley aged just sixteen years and fifty-three days, scoring a hat trick against Leeds United. A move to West Ham follows but he never starts a game for the Hammers and fades from the football scene, despite his early promise. Moffatt is last heard of when he makes the news for trying to marry a rat at sea, leading to a radical change in the nautical marriage laws.

May 1992: Cash-strapped Swansea have record signing Andy Bartram repossessed by the TSB bank after they fail to keep up with repayments on the loan taken out to sign him.

The manager of the Swansea branch of the bank, Martin Dagger, says, 'Their loss is the TSB's gain. He's a big, strong lad and we'll be looking to beef him up a bit and enter him in regional strongman contests. Plus, he's got a bit of a resemblance to Ross Kemp so we'll be aiming to exploit the lookalike market too.

Bartram says, 'It's not ideal, but I suppose this is the way football is these days,' before kissing the embroidered TSB badge on his freshly starched shirt and going off to make some tea.

August 1992: New Leyton Orient signing Shaun Britton gets off to a bad start in his first TV interview since joining the club. While making a wanking motion with his right hand and using a really sarcastic tone of voice, Britton tells reporters, 'Oh yes, I'm REALLY pleased to be playing for Orient – in fact, it's been a lifelong ambition. Mmmm, over the moon, totally, yeah.' A club official makes excuses for Britton's behaviour, explaining that the player is on tablets, but things don't improve on his debut, when he takes a dump in the Brisbane Road centre circle before kick-off.

March 1993: The Premier League table could soon take on a whole different shape if new FA proposals are passed. Plans are announced to replace the traditional 'league ladder' table with a large glutinous sphere, and match winners will be awarded weight instead of points.

FA spokesman Graham Kelly announces that 'The more wins a team clocks up, the more weight they'll be awarded, and the best team will slowly sink into the centre of the sphere. Relegated teams will appear close to the surface of the ball and will be shaved off at the end of the season.' Davies also reveals that the awarding of the league championship will be signified with a huge golden eagle bursting out of the sphere on the final day of the season, carrying the badge of the winning side the length and breadth of Britain.

The new system has been created by a London-based consultancy firm, at the cost of £140 million.

June 1993: Ipswich Town are forced to renovate Portman Road following a gig at the stadium by REM, after the pitch sinks 40ft below its usual level. REM singer Michael Stipe urges fans to jump up and down during 'Shiny Happy People' and, by the end of the song, the pitch level has dropped significantly. A spokesman says, 'We need to sink the rest of the stadium down as well, otherwise fans will be craning their necks trying to peer down at the match every week.'

August 1993: Wrexham's veteran winger Dai Evans is jailed for selling over £150,000 of counterfeit bank notes. Evans has developed a tidy sideline selling the notes to the club's young trainees, and is jailed for three years. The judge tells him, 'The final straw came when you began openly selling counterfeit money to fans during matches as you prepared to take corner kicks.'

November 1993: Watford defender Gudni Korg has his recent red card overturned after video evidence shows that he had began burying his way into the pitch at the time of the card being shown. An FA spokesman says, 'The laws of the game clearly state that the whole of the offending player's body must be above the surface of the pitch when the referee hands out the punishment. The video evidence shows that Korg was two-thirds submerged and, as such, he will not serve a suspension.'

Korg's whereabouts are unknown, since he tunnels his way out of Vicarage Road following the incident, and a full police manhunt is launched.

January 1994: The enigmatic and eccentric French design genius Phillipe Starck is hired by Charlton Athletic and tasked with the job of redesigning the Jimmy Seed Stand. Starck's modifications included replacing all plastic seating with tree stumps, creating a waterfall of tea lights down the steps and fitting the gents' urinals with miniature video screens of Richard Rufus blinking in slow motion.

Charlton manager Alan Curbishley says, 'There is always room in football for a design consciousness,' and announces that he plans to 'turn The Valley into a breathing, visceral art space.' Curbishley's next planned commission is a performance-art living sculpture featuring Shaun Newton and Mark Robson eating blades of grass, entitled *Pacified Soul/Absorbed/Goal/Mouth 1*.

March 1994: Arsenal midfielder Ray Parlour makes the shocking revelation that he changed his name as a teenager to avoid a clash with his then namesake. Parlour tells *Kick It Now* magazine, 'When I was sixteen, there was a tap-dancer on a TV talent show called Ray Hall who had the same name as me. There was always going to be confusion once I made it as a player so I thought, "Ray, what's bigger than a hall?" and it came to me – a parlour. So I did it.' Unfortunately, Parlour never made the name change official and faces a seven-year jail sentence for fraud.

May 1994: Fifteen thousand Carlisle United fans pack into Brunton Park to celebrate the news that hated central defender Shaun Goode has signed for Bournemouth in a £5,000 deal. Carlisle supporters spokesman Paul Lennon says, 'Goode's been a thorn in the team's side for five years. The reason so many people have shown up today is so that they can make sure the bastard's definitely going.'

September 1994: Scunthorpe striker Dean Godden pledges his support to Comic Relief by paying to have breast implants. Godden says, 'I've always had deposits of fat around my nipples, so I thought it would be a good idea to go the whole hog and get myself a full set.' The striker misses three crucial fixtures when he travels to Holland for the op, which is costing him £15,000 of his own cash. It is unclear as to how the stunt will benefit Comic Relief.

December 1994: Financially troubled Cardiff City aim to get more fans through the turnstiles by introducing a new cashback service from their back four. Supporters are able to enter the field of play at appropriate times, and any of the team's defenders, who will be playing with credit-card-authorisation machines strapped to their sides, will be able to hand out cash sums, with a maximum of £250 per fan. A spokesman for FIFA boss Sepp Blatter said, 'I don't know what Sepp thinks of this but, if it's got anything to do with cash, I'm sure he'll be delighted.'

March 1995: Highly rated youngster Keith Heald makes his debut for Sheffield Wednesday aged just 15 years and

113 days. Tipped as a future England captain when he first bursts on to the scene, an ankle injury ends his career prematurely, and he is last seen working part-time as a freelance scarecrow in Norfolk.

May 1995: Controversial animated non-league team Potters Bar Scrawlers finish top of their league at the first attempt. Created over the course of ten months by a team of Korean cartoonists, who also animate episodes of *The Simpsons*, the side faced abuse and protests from live-action opponents throughout the course of the season. Undaunted, the Scrawlers vowed to return after the summer with a whole host of new characters, including a striker with a nuclear boot and a goalkeeper who can expand himself like a blowfish. It doesn't end well for them, though, after FIFA boss Sepp Blatter has them erased using a special machine that he has built in his underground lair in Zurich.

August 1995: The Scottish FA clamps down on the attempts by a gang of local crack dealers to become the new sponsors of Livingston FC. The dealers, who later turn their attentions to Greenock Morton, planned to emblazon the slogan 'Have A Crack Attack' on the players' shirts, and saw the move as an ideal way to break the difficult teenage market. Spokesman Doddsy says, 'Livingston are a community club, and we desperately wanted our message to reach the community. But there's plenty of other ways.'

July 1995: Sky Sports, anxious to stay ahead in the race to bring fans the best coverage, unveil plans to use celebrity film directors during the soccer season. Their first approach is to veteran cult director David Lynch, who is invited to direct the season opener between Manchester United and Everton.

Lynch, who has never watched a football match in his life, is thrilled at the opportunity – when asked about his plans for the big game, he says he is considering the possibility of Paul Scholes experiencing a psychotic fugue towards the end of the first half. 'I also hope we can get a backwards midget to play the referee,' he enthusiastically adds. 'That would be kinda neat.'

Lynch also hopes to provide additional features for the Sky Sports Extra red-button service, including extreme close-up footage of Everton physio Chris Christmas extracting a tiny typed letter from under the fingernail of temperamental centre-forward Duncan Ferguson.

October 1995: Middlesbrough have a request to postpone their match with Bristol Rovers turned down by the FA after their excuse of 'It's a bit nippy for this time of year' isn't deemed worthy of postponement.

November 1995: Bosses of the Premier League plan to raise its profile by decorating the league table with tinsel and twinkling Christmas lights over the festive period. Throughout the year the table is kept in an aircraft hangar owned by the FA, and the teams' positions are changed by germ-free volunteers within minutes of matches ending, before fresh photographs of it are released to TV broadcasters. Safety officials are hoping to avoid a repeat of last month's minor firework disaster, when the relegation zone caught fire for ten minutes and Coventry City was almost completely destroyed.

December 1995: Instead of the traditional players' Christmas party, Oldham Athletic players, supporters and staff join forces to burn down the homes of local sex offenders.

January 1996: Fears grow for veteran midfielder Lee Bloom after he becomes trapped in the transfer window. Bloom, thirty-three, was in the process of completing a free transfer from Rochdale to Scunthorpe United when his shirt became snagged on a nail protruding from the window frame. Initial efforts to free him failed, with time running out as the window slowly closes ahead of the deadline at the end of the month.

Bloom's spirits remain high, though, as he is supplied with food and drink while friends and family maintain a round-the-clock vigil. However, an unnamed source says, 'We've not got long. The window is now just a few inches from his chin. If we don't save him this whole thing could lead to a complete unravelling of the Bosman.'

June 1996: Billionaire Microsoft boss Bill Gates buys the Premier League, with his £7.5 billion bid accepted by League Chief Executive Richard Scudamore after an all-night meeting in London. A delighted Gates unveils his plans for the future of the league to reporters the following morning, saying, 'I see a future in which football becomes an integrated, streamlined part of everyday life. It is the number-one sport in the world, as the World Cup proves, and we intend to implant a wafer-thin transmitter into the brain of every living person on the planet. These receivers will enable people to see live games in their own minds.'

Gates reveals he has already trademarked the name 'ThoughtSoccer' and believes that games created within the mind will lead to the phasing out of live games. 'Why would we need stadiums, or television broadcasts, or any of the paraphernalia associated with real soccer matches? In the future, you will simply think the match and it will happen.'

But following a seven-hour meeting with his technical team later that afternoon, Gates withdraws his bid and never speaks of football again.

August 1996: As Bradford unveil him at a press conference, Chilean striker Augustin Carmona causes a stir when he waves a pistol around and individually insults every reporter in the room. Sporting sunglasses and smoking a cigar, Carmona calls the *Sun*'s Neil Potter a 'creepy limey pussybag', threatening to give him a thousand paper cuts and spray him with vinegar if he writes anything negative about him or Bradford. After just two starts for the Bantams, it is discovered that Carmona is a pizza delivery man from Dewsbury called Ian Stringer, and his contract is terminated.

February 1997: A new report suggests that up to 80 per cent of Premier League players may have never have played professional football before signing for their clubs. The report claims that most players fake their CVs before sending them in to the clubs they're applying to play for. An unnamed insider at a top-flight club says, 'We know this sort of thing goes on but, weirdly, it usually works out OK.' The report comes shortly after an episode of an MTV celebrity prank show that featured all three members of Destiny's Child successfully signing for Fulham.

March 1997: Yeovil manager and amateur inventor Paul Ruskin claims he has created a footballing hologram that he says will soon take the place of real players, saving clubs millions of pounds. Ruskin travels to Switzerland to meet Sepp Blatter and discuss the new technology, but his hologram explodes on the plane due to cabin pressure, maiming eighteen passengers. A furious Blatter tries to berate Ruskin when they eventually meet, but the Yeovil boss silences him with his intergalactic space gun, which actually fires hot custard.

May 1997: In a surprising interview with *Shoot* magazine, Rolling Stones guitarist Keith Richards reveals he gave up a promising career in football 'because of drugs'. 'Basically, I couldn't get any,' complains the leather-faced guitar legend. 'I was an apprentice at Brentford, the Bees, and we'd train during the day, clean a few boots then I'd head on down to Chiswick at night to catch some blues. I was a great defender. Liked to get stuck in. Used a knife once or twice. Caught a ref round the head with a skull ring when I was thirteen.'

Richards says the lack of good-quality hash made him throw in the towel. 'In the sixties, apprentices were on three bob a week. I'd save it up to buy some decent puff. But no one at the club was selling the good Moroccan slabs. Bert the groundsman used to slip me a few leapers, and I know for a fact the chairman was dealing horse, but could I get some decent marijuana? It was very disappointing.'

Though building a decent reputation for its access to heroin, it was Brentford's neighbours, Queens Park Rangers, that offered the best cannabis in London. 'The weed at that gaff was the very, very best,' cackles Richards.

August 1997: Austrian international defender Jan Shittipants is forbidden from signing for Aberdeen by the Scottish FA as his name is deemed to be too rude. The league bosses put their foot down and invoke a little-known rule, which they originally introduced way back in 1901 when Stirling Albion caused a riot by fielding a goalkeeper named John McTits. Other foreign imports who have been turned away at the Scottish border because of the rule include Per Fukface, Dieter Clitt, Johann Poschbastard and Miekel Arsehol.

August 1997: Torquay United announce that they will be the first club to experiment with kicking off at 5.30am on a Sunday morning, following massive demand from their fans. The first early start comes in late August of 1997 but, half an hour into their first dawn match, the death of Princess Diana is announced and the match is abandoned due to mass hysteria. An FA inquiry later rules that early morning Sabbath kick-offs are unlucky.

October 1997: The Kwik Fit Terrace Twat award is launched, in recognition of all those pricks who get right on everyone's tits at football grounds the length and breadth of the land. The inaugural winner of the monthly award is Swindon Town fan Phil Belper, for the crazy football-shaped hat that he wears to all of the team's home and away matches. Subsequent winners include Raith Rovers fan Neil Glossop, who has a selection of plastic trumpets, and eighty-six-year-old Carlisle United supporter Norman Fairley, who invariably gets a jelly baby stuck in his windpipe each week and ends up being attended to by the St John Ambulance team.

February 1998: Highly-rated youngster Tommy McCrossan makes his Dundee United debut at the age of eight, after signing up to the club's youth academy when he was only eleven months old. Many feel that the young striker has been thrown in at the deep end too quickly, especially as he cries for six whole weeks after the match. Sadly, it all goes wrong for McCrossan, who fades from the scene after a move to Arsenal, aged twelve. He is last seen living in London, where he allows rich businessmen to hit him in the face with a ping-pong bat for fast cash.

May 1998: Legendary West Ham steward Clive Jenny, believed to be the rudest steward in British history, ends his glittering forty-three-year career at Upton Park. It is estimated that, during his long tenure, he single-handedly turned away 546,000 people for 'not having the correct documentation', including Bobby Moore, Harry Redknapp and the late Ronnie Kray. Jenny is finally sacked after subjecting Sir Trevor Brooking to a nine-day kidnapping ordeal for showing the wrong-colour ticket at the entrance to the directors' buffet. He is given an OBE in 2001.

June 1998: Swansea City close down their brand-new website after an online poll to find their greatest ever player is won by Rambo. An investigation is launched but the club announce that there are no immediate plans to cancel the presentation of the award to actor Sylvester Stallone, who will appear dressed as his famous character on the final day of the season.

August 1998: Newcastle United star Nolberto Solano launches an angry attack against the makers of an unofficial website devoted to his trumpet. Writing on his own official website, dedicated to the instrument, Solano says, 'My trumpet is my small metal wife. Anyone who wishes to promote or debate my wife in public with the permission of neither of us must perish with cysts. Cysts.'

November 1998: New guidelines and clampdowns and that are called for as the BBC's *Panorama* uncovers horrifying evidence of mascot abuse throughout every level of the game. The programme reveals that, in Scotland, Brechin's Hedgy the Hedgehog is kept in a skip in between matches while being fed rotting cabbages. Worst of all is the plight of Hartlepool's H'Angus the Monkey, who would have to visit the homes of season-ticket holders after every home defeat and lick their doorsteps clean at gunpoint.

December 1998: Instead of the traditional boozy players' Christmas party, Arsenal's players spend an evening at a gallery, studying a selection of works by art students. They then move on to a wine-tasting session in the City, where they arrogantly deride the quality of life in England and laugh at how so many French players have been paid fortunes to play in the Premier League and yet their national team remains far superior to their English counterpart.

January 1999: Spanish striker Enrique González wants three contracts before he'll sign for Middlesbrough, owing to the fact that he's a schizophrenic with three different personalities. He says, 'I am Enrique the football star, Enrique the refuse collection man and Enrique the poet and womaniser. If you want to sign the football star, then you must pay for all three of us. We are as one.' Boro decline to sign him, and González is later jailed for having sex with a bookshop dustbin in Valencia.

March 1999: Spanish misfit Marcelino has had the last laugh at those who branded his spell at Newcastle United a waste of time. During his four years at the club, the defender made just nineteen appearances for the Magpies and was savagely criticised by the club's supporters, but he has now revealed that he was spending his time single-handedly building a speedboat, which he has donated to the city.

Marcelino tells Spanish magazine *El Nautico*, 'Although I could not always play, I wanted to give something back to the fine people of my adopted city. It is my eternal gift to them.'

A spokesman for Newcastle City Council says, 'It's a noble gesture, but one which we are sadly unable to accept.' This is believed to be due to the fact that Marcelino has carved 'Fuck Your Toon' along both sides of the boat.

July 1999: Sepp Blatter unveils his latest scheme to spice up the Champions League, only days after his 'kestrels for refs' plan collapses in a cloud of allergies and lawsuits. Blatter announces that he wants opposing captains to pretend to be old friends and feign surprise at seeing each other when they go to the centre circle for the coin toss. He says, 'Think how nice that would be for everyone. Everyone loves a beautiful reunion.'

September 1999: Former Wimbledon manager Joe Kinnear reveals that he's been invisible for the past three months, claiming that he bought a second-hand invisibilisation machine with his compensation payout, and says he's never felt better.

He says, 'I've been doing a bit of scouting for a couple of old mates and spending the rest of my time on the golf course. I'm getting a perm this afternoon. Nobody's got a fucking clue.' Kinnear confesses he is in no hurry to return to management.

October 1999: Manchester United fans think about things the most, according to a pointless new poll carried out by a doomed mobile-phone provider. The poll, which appears in several tabloid newspapers and is discussed for five hours on Talksport, finds that the average supporter of the

Red Devils thinks about lots of things, while the nearest contenders, Charlton fans, think about a few things. Most Spurs fans think about nothing.

November 1999: Financially strapped League Two clubs come up with a revolutionary ground-sharing scheme involving two separate football games taking place at the same time on the same pitch.

'We came up with the concept when it became clear that so few League Two games were selling out,' revealed Football League Commercial Director Stewart Thomson. 'Clubs need to get more fans through the turnstiles. They need to try to save administrative and housekeeping costs. Even things like floodlighting can be a real headache when the electricity bill lands on the chairman's doormat.'

In brief, the new scheme will involve four teams kicking off on the same ground at the same time. 'In effect, there'll be one referee, two assistant referees and forty-four players. Fans from four different clubs will pack into the stands, creating a terrific atmosphere with good-natured rivalry. It's going to be really exciting to watch, with four teams fighting over two balls.'

December 1999: Sheffield United players threaten to go on strike after manager Neil Warnock cancels their Christmas party, replacing it with an illustrated lecture delivered by Warnock himself in which he puts forward his plans for an armed invasion of Belgium in the following pre-season. Meanwhile, instead of the traditional boozy players' Christmas party, the Wimbledon squad face something very different indeed. 'Manager Egil Olsen is sealing the entire squad in a large cube and leaving them in the middle of the New Forest... no one's quite sure why,' explained a Dons spokesperson.

THE SECRET SOCCER SUPERSTAR'S MYSTERY PLAYERS (PART TWO)

Here's some more secrets about some of the world's top players that are so secret that I can't even tell you who they're about. That's why they call me the Secret Soccer Superstar...

Who is the Caribbean international who lives alone with life-size dummies of his team-mates?

Which goal-shy striker plans to reveal a T-shirt reading 'I Be the King of All Romance' when he finally hits the back of the net?

Who is the top European manager who only conducts transfer negotiations through a mask made from the face of a stuffed ape?

Which former Premier League boss is a masked club DJ and spins groove at Essex warehouse parties under his pseudonym, 'DJ Evil Horse'?

Who is the Irish international who can't help asking teenage supporters if he can squeeze their zits for them?

Which Welsh international tries to go to training every morning in his hang glider but always crash-lands in his next-door neighbour's garden?

Who is the manager who woke up next to a severed bear's head when he refused to throw an important top-of-the-table clash? The rest of the bear was later discovered in the passenger seat of his Porsche Boxster.

Which relegation-threatened side have promised to give the players their own weight in marzipan if they beat the drop?

Which Italian international will only travel to away games if he can get there by rowing his rubber dinghy?

Who is the full-back with a dream of packing it all in and becoming a weather forecaster?

Why have a particular club announced huge season-ticket price rises? Could it have something to do with an upcoming child-slavery court case?

Who is the Premier League manager who doesn't trust other road users and travels everywhere through a network of underground tunnels he's built himself between his home and the training ground?

Which foreign full-back doesn't understand English money and tries to pay for everything with kisses?

Which European chairman leases his club from a local toy factory, as part of a deal that keeps him in free jigsaws for life?

Which imposing striker won't be getting a contract renewal unless he drops his habit of non-stop farting in the dressing room at half-time?

Which under-fire boss has a secret other job? He dresses

up as a masked superhero and does door-to-door dog haircuts.

Who is the international manager who gives his team talks in a parrot-style squawking language that he's invented himself?

Who is the Welsh international with the word 'Whales' tattooed on his arm?

Which millionaire striker has had an alternative universe built into a wardrobe in his mansion?

Who is the foreign import who is actually English? He couldn't get signed up as a teenager so went abroad and changed his name, and now he's on £180,000 a week!

Who is the giant defender who can't sleep unless he's curled up into a ball?

Who is the player who used a special-effects squib to make it look as though he had been shot during a match, netting himself 15 per cent of his paymaster's £2 million windfall after a massive bet was placed on it to happen.

Which Spanish midfielder is really 60 per cent woman? He gets away with it by strapping his tits into his armpits.

Which retired England international hasn't left the house for four months, and sits around watching CCTV footage of the inside of his own pants while scratching himself with a claw?

Which Scottish striker is banned from his local petrol station for drinking unleaded straight out of the pump?

Who is the pint-sized winger who spends six hours a day on a stretching rack in a desperate bid to increase his height?

Who is the European chairman who arranged for his

club's retractable pitch to roll out of the stadium during a match, taking the players with it? He got paid a very tasty £800,000 bung, and the pitch was later found 75 miles away by the coast, with the oblivious players still carrying on with the game.

Who is the international defender who insists on humming the whole of the album *A Trick of the Tail* by Genesis before every game?

Which Manchester United legend always wore an extra pair of socks – on his testicles?

Who is the former Champions League-winning striker who would spend the morning before an away game hitting himself with a bible? He also once advertised for willing virgins who were prepared to sacrifice themselves in his underground temple at his club's stadium.

THE ALDERMAN AND THE CHARITY FOOTBALL MATCH

I went up to Stockton a while ago, for the Alderman's annual charity football match. It was Town Hall officials, the Alderman and all his cronies versus minor celebrities like myself – there was me, Stephen Tompkinson, Big Business Steph from *BBC Breakfast News*, Me Mark Page, who used to be on Radio One, and Biffy Clyro, the pop star. It was all to raise money for the dreary, gloomy kids and their parents.

So, the Town Clerk, he's manager of the council team and the Alderman's managing my celebrity team, and it's a half-decent game, actually. Biffy Clyro's a bit useless, though – he just stands wide on the wing, drawing on his face – no good to anyone.

Tompkinson's a useful centre-half, but he's getting a bit fed up with the antics of the vicar (who's got a twitch and stinks of bleach) – he's a really physical player. Wiry, like Peter Crouch, but not quite as tall – really difficult to play against. Treating it like it's a cup final, even though it's just a charity thing – really getting stuck in.

It's a tight game and, just before half-time, Big Business Steph from the breakfast news hacks down the Chief Planning Officer in the box and gives away a penalty. Bleachy vicar takes it and it's 1-0 at half time.

The Alderman gives us the team talk – he tells Biffy to go and wash his fucking face and tells Big Business Steph to stop being so physical. Then he turns to me and he says, 'Robert! What's going on, Robert? You're not the Robert we were expecting, Robert. You're one-paced, lethargic, Robert. Get a grip, Robert.'

I didn't say anything because, to be honest, I knew he was right; the game was just passing me by. It remains a tight game and we're down to the last two minutes and it's still 1-0. Clyro's still stood on the touchline, drawing on his face like some kind of prick. I mean, we're basically playing with ten men – he's a fucking liability but, to be honest, he was the biggest star we had and we needed him to get the crowds in.

Couple of minutes left and I'm hacked down by the Chief Planning Officer. The trainer rushes on with a bag and the magic sponge and some of that spray you get from Boots, and I don't know if I can carry on. He says, 'Nonsense,' and I say, 'No, Geoff, really – I'm in too much pain. I think I'm finished for the match.'

My team-mates all gradually gather around. They lean in, and I look up to see Big Business Steph and Me Mark Page and Bernie Slaven, the ex-Middlesbrough striker, all staring down at me. Suddenly, they all separate. There he is, stood looking down at me – the Alderman. He's taken his fleece off and he's wearing the tightest mustard polo neck you could imagine, and a nice checked trilby.

What does everyone start chanting? Of course – 'Kiss the Alderman, kiss the Alderman, kiss the Alderman...' The Alderman leans his face right over me and he says, 'Help us, Robert. You're our only hope, Robert.'

Then his lips softly clasp on to mine and he slowly moistens my mouth with his saliva. I swear I've never been kissed like that before. It was like electricity passing through my body. I was literally straight up on my feet and, from the free kick, I ran straight at their defence. I nutmegged the vicar and I did a one-two with Big Business Steph before gliding past the Head of Child Protection and smashing it into the net. Final kick of the match.

Big Business Steph lifted me right up above her head, and it felt as good as a victory, equalising right at the end like that. AND we managed to raise £189 for the daft kids. What a story... and what a kiss!

IT'S MUM-AND-DAD MAYHEM IN KIDDIE-LEAGUE BRITAIN

The footballing authorities are desperate to clamp down on the bad touchline behaviour of parents of school-age players – anyone who's been near an organised kids match knows exactly what we're talking about. Sadly, though, efforts to get grown-ups to clean up their act don't seem to be working.

Here are some of the more shocking incidents that all took place at the Under-8 level of the game over the past month...

A furious mum drugged by paramedics after she started foaming at the mouth when her son was tackled from behind. She was later sectioned.

An enraged dad burying himself alive on the touchline as a protest after his son was denied a penalty.

A fight breaking out between eighteen parents of players on two different teams. In the end, the brawl spilled over on to the pitch, with the kids moving to the touchline to encourage their parents. This then led to another mass brawl.

A gang of parents storming the pitch inside a massive Chinese dragon and chasing the referee all the way back to his car after a row over a foul throw.

The Albanian mafia casually handing out leaflets offering to act as agents for up-and-coming young players along with bespoke match-fixing and referee assassination services.

WHEN WILL THIS MADNESS END?

TOM JONES'S GOLD EXTRAVAGANCE

I once met Gary Lineker – I went out one night drinking with Gary Lineker and Sir Tom Jones. You know, the Welsh Honker, the Sex Bomb. But he's a lovely man – in fact, they both are, and I had a lovely night.

But I got to thinking that these two have got some serious cash. Not like me, because I'm not a millionaire or anything. And I thought to myself that they're nice people, because you get some boastful celebrities, showy ones – a lot of footballers are like that. They're all, 'I've got the Bentley, I've got this, I've got this, I've got this...' But not Gary and Sir Tom.

So I said to Sir Tom, 'You're with friends here. Come on, tell us about something that you spent a load of money on; something extravagant that you love and that you don't want to apologise for. I'm not going to tell anyone.'

He says, 'No, no, no – no way,' so I said, 'Awww, go on, Tom. I'd love it if you told me. You know, if ever, one day, I had loads of money, I'd love to spend it on some big indulgence.' But he stood firm, saying, 'No, no, no, I don't like stuff like that getting out.'

I said, 'Please, please, please, Sir Tom. I beg of you. Please tell me.'

So he says, 'Alright... I got a fucking gold plane.'

I said, 'What do you mean, gold?' He says, 'Fucking gold taps, gold walls, gold seats, gold thread in the carpets. A fucking gold plane.'

I was gobsmacked – didn't even get the chance to ask if he takes it out and flies it. I don't suppose he does – it's probably too heavy to take off.

JUST WHO ARE THE FA'S BANNING SQUAD?

Whenever one of your team's players picks up a ban after being called in front of an FA disciplinary committee, do you ever find yourself wondering who the anonymous figures on that committee actually are? Hmmmm, yes, us too.

We've done some research into these tinpot charlies who hand out the bans; officials who have usually had no experience of the game at a professional level. But just who are they? Here's a typical disciplinary line-up...

STUART WEATHERMOTHER (aged 89): Deputy Vice District Secretary, Latchley FA. Once banned a Sunday-league goalkeeper for eleven months for blowing a kiss to his wife at half-time. Lives alone with an inflatable dummy of Sepp Blatter, which he likes to dress as an Austrian goat-herding girl.

GORDON TRILL (aged 97): Under-secretary (seconded), Smenton FA. Known locally as the Terminator and hands out lifetime bans like the Easter Bunny hands out eggs. In 2004, he suspended himself from his role for eight months after he caught himself thinking about tennis during Wimbledon fortnight.

LESTER PIGGLES (aged 112): Sub-postmaster, Chuffney FA. In his spare time, Lester likes to re-enact famous executions, and sits in judgment in an electric chair that he likes to punish himself with. Once tried to fine an amateur referee £1 million for not sending off a player who had died during an Over-40s pre-season friendly.

NIGEL FARTHANDLER (aged 76): Head of Domination / Re-education Minister, Pimton FA. Regarded as a 'bright young thing' in FA circles. Famously tried to ban fictional comic-strip footballer Roy Race when he signed Spandau Ballet's Kemp brothers for Melchester Rovers, after the paperwork failed to arrive at FA headquarters.

JEREMY CORBYN'S CREATIVE AGENCY

I got off the train at King's Cross on my way to record the podcast, and I was early so I decided to nip into a café and get myself a bacon sandwich. Who should be sat there? Jeremy Corbyn.

He's sitting there with a plate of barbecue spare ribs in front of him, which I thought was a bit odd because (a) it was only ten o'clock in the morning, and (b) he's a vegetarian, apparently. And it was just the ribs that were left – it looked as though a dog had sucked the meat off them.

So I says, 'Alright there, Jez. They your bones there, are they?'

He says, 'NO! They're Billy Bragg's. He's gone for a shit.'

Sure enough, a couple of seconds later, Billy Bragg comes out of the gents, and he shouts, 'YOU CAN'T TAKE IT WIV YA, CAN YA? EH? KNOW WHAT I MEAN?' To, like, nobody in particular.

Bragg sits down and he looks across at me, and he says, 'Alright, Treacle?' Between the two of them, they've got a load of sheets of paper and coloured pencils strewn all over the place, so they're up to something.

I said, 'What's this, lads – you planning the 2020 election campaign?'

Corbyn says, 'No! It's our day off! We're working on a side project today. We've launched a creative agency, providing tender ethical solutions in a cruel and unfeeling world.' He was getting a bit agitated at this stage and he has a little toot on a bright red inhaler that he carries around with him.

So I asked them, 'What are you working on, then?'

and Billy Bragg says, 'We're pitching for the John Lewis Christmas advert,' and Corbyn adds, 'Yes, as a Cuban-style workers' co-operative, John Lewis is exactly the kind of friendly capitalist organisation that we're aiming to break into.'

I said, 'Alright, what's your pitch, then? Have you got a storyline for this Christmas advert, then?'

Corbyn got all animated at this. 'Yes. Yes, we do. I will tell it to you now.' Billy says, 'Can I do a bit of it, Jez?'

'No, Bill. No, we've already been through this. You can operate the PowerPoint clicker if you can get your timing right beforehand.'

'Alright, Jez,' says Billy. 'I'll keep practising. I'll keep practising.'

Corbyn says, 'OK, here we go,' and he starts speaking quietly, because he doesn't want anyone else in the café to overhear his idea and nick it.

'It's the morning after a nuclear holocaust. A single mother emerges from her impromptu home-made shelter and ventures out into the street. Death and destruction is everywhere. She looks across at the town square and, to her amazement, the Christmas tree has remained intact.

He goes on, 'Suddenly, a sleigh pulls into view. On it is Ded Moroz, the Russian version of Father Christmas. He approaches and strokes her face before kissing her softly 'pon the lips.'

Billy Bragg says, 'WE MIGHT DO A CGI THING AT THIS POINT, WHERE OUR EYES TURN INTO CARTOON HEARTS!' Corbyn says, 'I don't think the cartoon hearts are a good idea, Bill.'

I asked them, 'What happens next, then?' and Corbyn says, 'Ded Moroz removes his hood and beard to reveal that he's actually... Vladimir Putin!'

I say, 'Shit!' and Billy says, 'Yeah, that's what I said when Jez came up with it. Amazing, innit?'

Corbyn says, 'I think you'll find that it's heart-warming AND informative, with the slightest nod towards condemning the vile, capitalist fuckfest that is the modern British Christmas!' before having another little puff on his inhaler.

So I asked them, "What's the soundtrack to it, then?' because the song is always really important in the John Lewis ads, and Billy says, 'Yeah, I'm singing that. It's a gentle, slowed-down version of "Part of the Union" by The Strawbs. And then he sang a bit, a cappella. 'Me guitar's at the menders,' he says.

After he's finished, Corbyn says, 'Right, fuck off – we're due at the John Lewis head office in half an hour and I need to finish off colouring in this bar chart before we go.' I just made me excuses and left.

I didn't have the heart to tell them that John Lewis had already made their Christmas advert by then.

GANGS OF THE EPL - THE ARSENAL GANG

I went to see the Boro play the Arsenal last week, down at the Emirates. I get there nice and early and there was a very nice Tesco by the away end and I bought a couple of Scotch eggs and a massive strawberry Yoplait – you know, the ones that are about a foot tall.

Now, I'm about two or three hours early, because I've got what's called a Triple A pass – that stands for 'Access All Areas'. It's exactly the same pass that, say, Tom Cruise or Barry Cryer would get if they were going to the Arsenal match. It's the top pass, and I get it because I'm a superstar celebrity who's been on the telly and I've had heart problems.

So, anyway, this is about the gangs of the EPL. I get there early for a sniff around and, in the Emirates you get to the different floors using a lift. I'm in the lift on my own, and I see that the very bottom button is for the VIP car park at the very bottom of the stadium. So I thought I'd go and have a look at all the flashy cars in the car park, because I'm not bothered about meeting people and having hot dogs and that. I'm more into machines than men.

I'm down there, having a look at all the lovely cars and, suddenly, I hear a sort of hushed whispering. 'Psh, psh, psh, hsh, hsh, hsh, psh, psh,' – that sort of thing. I look over next to a pillar and, beside a white Porsche Panamera, registration number THEO 14, there's Danny Welbeck, Theo Walcott and Alex Oxlade-Chamberlain.

They can't see me but I can see them – they're wearing what you can only call Peaky Blinder outfits, from that

BBC2 show. Tweed waistcoats, woollen trousers, cloth caps and big hobnail boots.

I'm near enough to hear them, and Theo is saying, 'Right – I've had enough of that Spurs gang saying nasty things about us. Unfavourable things, hurtful things, like we don't know how to use cash machines or that our mams still do our washing.'

Ooooh, I thought to myself, he's got a strop on, hasn't he? Just at this point, Santi Cazorla walks by on his way to the changing rooms, and he goes, 'HOLA, THEO! YOU WANT TO COME TO MY BANANA AND LIQUID TAPAS PARTY TONIGHT? IT'S WELL BENT!'

Oxlade says, 'No, we don't – piss off, Sanity Pants,' and Theo says, 'Take your bullshit to another person or group of people. We don't allow pigeon chests in our gang, anyway – it's not a body shape we particularly appreciate.' So Carzola says, 'OK, HOLA!' and off he goes.

Theo carries on. 'Now, they've had the early kick-off today – Spurs against the Matt Damons... Bournemouth, so I reckon Harry Kane will be back at his mam's now, for his tea and to get his chin polished. I say that, after the match, we sneak out without telling Mr Wenvenger, go to his mam's and shout at him from the car, "Hey, Chinny. Chinny drives a Mini. Hey, where'd you get that chin – the butcher's off-cuts bin? Mr Giroud is beautiful – you look like a fucking turnip farmer!"' Then he says, 'Now, my new car is so fast that, if his dad comes out, we can be in France before he's got to the end of his drive.'

Danny chips in and says, 'What if he's... what if... what if it's a... long driveway and he... he... has... has an intercom?'

Theo says, 'Well, we can press the button and say, "Delivery for Harry Kane," and, when they ask what it is, we can say it's a chin drainage and polishing system, or we could just shout, "Fuck off, farmer boy!" into the microphone part of the unit.'

Anyway, then I belched – I couldn't help it, because I'd had my Yoplait on top of the Scotch eggs. So Theo shouts, 'Come out, come out, whoever you are. It's a private club! What do you want, little bald bloke?'

So I say, 'Alright, alright, I'm just looking for my car,' and Oxlade says, 'Oh god, he's from the North of England. What sort of car is it – a Fiat Panda? Hoh, hoh, hoh, hoh, hoh, hoh, hoh.' And Theo says, 'Probably a Matchbox model car. I hope you've kept the packaging, as it'll be worth more and you can sell it to pay for food or gas and electric.'

At this point, Aitor Karanka, the Middlesbrough manager, walks past, and I think he might save me, so I go, 'Alright, Aitor!' and he goes, 'Urrrrrrrrrrrrrrrrrrrrrrrrrrrrrrrr… nice car,' and then he walks off, which is no good to me.

Theo says, 'Like I said, this is a private club, and you can't join us unless you know the secret password.'

So I say, 'Well, it's Peaky Gooners, isn't it?'

'He's nailed it,' says Oxlade. 'I'm upset,' says Danny. 'I can feel an injury coming on.'

'Oh, that's just great,' says Theo. 'We can't go on Operation Chin Chin with our security compromised!'

So I say, 'Look, I've got an offer for you, lads. I know both the main Spurs gangs – I know the Sherwoods and the White Harts. They're planning something big against your gang. I could find out the details for you, but I want something in return.'

'What is it?' says Theo.

I said, 'You make sure that Arsenal don't score today.' So they looked at each other, and then Theo says, 'Right – it's a DEAL!'

So the rest is history. He was good to his word, they didn't score: 0-0 – great result for the Boro, and now both Spurs gangs and Theo's gang think I'm working for them.

Wonder what'll happen next…

FOOTBALLERS IN THE WILD (PART FOUR)

Here's the final bunch of the best player sightings from the Footballers in the Wild section of our podcast.

BRYAN OVIEDO scooting down Oxford Street, wearing a pair of those Heelie shoes and singing Snoop Dogg's 'Gin and Juice'.

Crystal Palace owner STEVE PARISH sitting on the bonnet of his car, talking on his mobile, overheard saying, 'You're not going to believe what that cleaning lady's left in the bogs now, Ray!'

MARCOS ALONSO eating a taco and chatting about the price of racehorses to a ventriloquist's doll.

JUNIOR STANISLAS in a library in Bournemouth, carrying what looked like a bag of blood with the word 'donkey' written on it.

BRAD FRIEDEL at a Portsmouth golf-course clubhouse, asking how much it would cost to hire six 'bats' for the afternoon.

DANNY SIMPSON in the back of a taxi, telling the driver he'd give him fifteen grand if he'd crash into a tree because he wanted to see what it felt like.

JAMES MILNER sitting at the top of a children's slide, possibly crying.

KAKÁ on the back seat of a taxi – £45 for the clean-up bill.

JOHN HARTSON in his local newsagents, cancelling his papers because he reckons he's about to sign for Barcelona.

WAYNE ROONEY outside a leisure centre in Knutsford, trying (and failing) to put a sweatband over his fat head.

NACHO MONREAL in the back of a taxi, listening to Simply Red and claiming to have written most of their songs over the last twenty years.

JONATHAN WALTERS in Derby city centre, going the wrong way up a one-way street on a BMX, pulling wheelies and scaring old people by making motorbike noises when he rides past them.

RUUD GULLIT in a bingo hall in Cricklewood. Every time the caller says, 'Two little ducks,' Gullit starts quacking, then falls off his chair in hysterics.

FABIO BORINI outside a cave, asking a hermit if he could come in because he said the weather was making him nervous.

GEOFFREY COSTA coming out of the toilets in Nando's, holding his hands out and shouting, 'They're clean. Come and check 'em if you want.'

LUIS SUÁREZ getting out of a helicopter in a field near Jodrell Bank, then hitting the ground and crawling on his belly as if someone was trying to shoot him.

GYLFI SIGURDSSON in the back of a taxi, telling the

driver that he's thinking about quitting football and starting a company that helps people in comas to wake up.

ALAN CURBISHLEY on the roof of Charlton's stadium, being asked what he was doing by a copper. He said he was getting his ball back.

TONY ADAMS in the back of a taxi, trying to pretend that he's actually a piano teacher, and boasting that he makes a million quid a year from it.

MOUSSA SISSOKO having his dinner in a pub with his agent, who is patiently trying to explain to him why he can't sign for Wembley.

TROY DEENEY'S dentist's mum's cousin's dentist telling a florist that Deeney will sign for whichever club will pay for him to do a day-release hypnotism course at college.

PAOLO DI CANIO getting on a plane to Nigeria with a couple of large sacks under his arm. He was also carrying a massive packet of cream crackers.

SERGIO BUSQUETS in the back of a taxi in London, practising a cockney accent and calling his hands his 'china mugs'.

JORDAN HENDERSON throwing pebbles up at the window of the boardroom at Anfield, shouting, 'Yoo hoo, can you let us in? I've forgotten me key!'

EDEN HAZARD in the middle of London, offering to buy a baseball cap from an American tourist. The tourist chased him away.

PELÉ in the back of a taxi, tipping Wigan for the Premier League title this year and saying that Steve Bruce is a 'hot potato', before touching his own chest and making a sizzling noise.

DARREN ANDERTON in his new role as a mystery shopper for Superdrug.

ROBBIE SAVAGE in Cardiff, cradling a doll version of himself and asking it if it wanted any nuts.

BACARY SAGNA in a Manchester bowling alley with a really short man – they scored eighty-six points between them.

JORDY CLASIE coming out of a travel agents in Southampton, wearing a sombrero and carrying some finger cymbals.

DAVID BENTLEY selling his used fishing equipment on a shopping channel at 5am.

CESC FABREGAS in the back of a taxi, telling the driver that he's happy at Chelsea because he gets loads of free sweets.

JOE LEDLEY wading into the Thames with a giant net and a copy of the *Sunday Sport*.

JAMES McCLEAN in the back of a taxi, telling the driver that he wants to sign for a League Two team because it'll make him look like a world-beater and help him win the Ballon D'or.

DJIBRIL CISSÉ on a Ryanair flight to Oslo, sporting a new tattoo on his face that says 'Let's Have a Nudie Pool Party!'

ERIK LAMELA buying a gift set of jams in Hackney. He said he definitely didn't want apricot because he knew someone who'd died from it.

JORDAN RHODES in the back of a taxi, telling the driver that, twice a month, he feels like 'fucking the whole thing off and going to work on an oil rig.'

LEIGHTON BAINES coming out of a butcher's shop, licking his lips and carrying a bag of tripe.

EMILE HESKEY modelling in a life-drawing class, holding up a hand-scrawled sign that read 'Extra £30 if you want me to speak about football'. No one stumped up.

MAROUANE FELLAINI running along a wall in Salford Quays, wearing a pair of wings, and trying to fly when he jumped off the end of the wall.

DANNY WELLBECK in the back of a taxi, telling the driver that he's not bothered if he can't get into the Arsenal team because it'll give him more time to play *Tetris*.

PATRICK VAN AANHOLT and JACK RODWELL crossing the road near the Stadium of Light while carrying a large pane of glass. Then a bloke on a motorbike crashed straight through it.

YOUNÈS KABOUL in a shopping precinct in Watford, trying to balance a beer mat on the end of his nose.

LEROY FER checking into a hotel, but giving his name as Spoony Boobfinder.

CASPER, I LOVE YOU (PART TWO)

We rejoin the story just after the Fat Lass has booted Casper through the air after seeing him dancing across the black-and-white tiled floor of the kitchen and almost triggering a fit.

After she launched the snake across the kitchen, she managed to shout, 'Steve, help me!' – of course, Steve runs into the kitchen, assuming she's shit her knickers and wants him to wipe her with the dirty dishcloth.

He immediately sees that she's fully clothed in her towelling wear and struggling with her balance, so he puts his arms around her. 'It's alright, love,' he says, 'calm down. It's just one of them daft fits you have 'cos of your haemoglobin content. Have a seat and I'll get you a glass of salted water to bring your blood pressure up and a sugar lump for your hypoglycaemia.'

The Fat Lass sits down and she's dribbling a bit. Not thinking, because he's got it in his hand, he wipes her mouth with the dirty dishcloth – leaves a little bit of cack on her lips, but she doesn't notice.

But Steve notices something – namely, the lifeless Casper, who's lying on the kitchen surface. Immediately, he knows that something unusual has happened, because Casper isn't allowed on the kitchen surfaces because of his spewing and that. Let's be honest, he's hardly able to climb up there, anyway, unless the Fat Lass has got her leggings and bandages and that drying on the clothes horse in front of the kitchen bench.

Steve goes over to the snake. 'What are you doing up there, you silly plonker, Rodney?' he says as he picks him up, but Casper is colder than he should be. He's not moving either, not at all; he's like a dead weight in Steve's arms.

'Casper!' says Steve. 'Casper, what's happened? Oh my god, Casper!'

He puts his ear to Casper's chest to see if he can hear a heartbeat, but it's really difficult because the Fat Lass's foot is twitching and kicking the baking trays that are slotted in the gap between the cabinets. DING, DING, DING, DING, DING. Also, she's got Chris Evans on the radio, who's making monkey noises – something to do with Wednesday Wacky Wildlife Klub he does, or something.

Steve's beginning to cry – he realises that there's something really wrong here. All he can think to do, because Casper is so cold, is to run him under the hot tap and see if that helps. He turns the hot tap on but, as soon as it comes on, he realises that it's far too hot, because the Fat Lass has been washing her bandages.

'Sorry, Casper! I'm sorry! Sorry!' cries Steve, but he swears he sees a tiny little movement around Casper's neck, like a little swallowing motion. 'Casper, you're alive!' he shouts. 'Hang on in there and I'll get you to hospital.'

He wraps Casper around his neck and he shakes the Fat Lass. 'Love, love, I've got to get Casper to the hospital – where are the car keys?' But she's not responding – she just keeps on kicking the baking trays. So he looks for his keys but he can't find them. 'Fuck it,' he thinks. 'I'll take the clown car.'

It's a typical circus clown's car – slightly square in shape, big wheels, yellow and bright red in colour, big parping horn on the front, which he honks all the way throughout the mile-long journey to the vet hospital. HONK, HONK, HONK.

'Casper's not well!' HONK, HONK, HONK. 'Out the way! Casper's not well!' HONK, HONK. All the people on the pavement, as he goes by, are pointing at Steve and singing, 'HE'S GOT A HAAAAIIIR ISLAAAAND! A HAAAAIIIR ISLAAAAND!'

Anyway, his steering wheel comes off at the lights, so he has to put it back in, and there's smoke billowing out of the arse end of the car. When he finally arrives at the vet's, all the doors fall off, but Steve hardly notices.

He rushes in and plonks Casper down in reception, and says, 'Please, please help me. Something's wrong. I've just found him like this, lying on the kitchen surface, next to the Homepride plain-flour jar.' The thing about the flour was extra information that he didn't need to give, but he's panicking and he thinks it might help somehow.

The vet's at reception and he immediately picks Casper up – as he does so, a little bit of spew dribbles out of Casper's mouth. A sign of life. Steve can't help but put a big smile on. 'That's my Casper. Come on, Casper, you've got to fight!'

The vet takes him straight into the surgery with a nurse and, as they go, the vet says over his shoulder, 'Looks like he's been kicked or hit with something blunt – he's bleeding.'

Steve realises what's happened and, under his breath, he growls, 'You bastard. You large bastard.'

To be continued…

A HISTORY
OF FOOTBALL

PART FIVE
THE NEW MILLENNIUM

January 2000: The FA announces controversial plans to build a new academy on Mars, in a project headed up by Howard Wilkinson. The former Leeds boss says, 'If there is life on Mars, surely it's the duty of the FA to harness it and bring on a new generation that can win us the World Cup once again?' Wilkinson aims to open the academy in 2009, once he has recruited a team of space warriors to wipe out any Martians who might get in the way of planning permission and other local administration difficulties.

March 2000: Carlisle United bosses are criticised after trying something a bit different for their half-time entertainment during a home FA Cup tie against Newport County. Professor Gunther von Hagens, performing a live autopsy on Jeff Caldicott – earlier voted the club's greatest player of all time – is regarded by some as unsuitable for a family football match, mainly due to the nudity of both von Hagens AND Caldicott.

June 2000: Top-earning players who have outdone each other with faster and more expensive cars turn to a new way of boosting their egos – caravans. An increasing number of big Premier League names are seen turning up for training pulling a touring caravan behind them, and they spend their spare time comparing models and shopping for accessories. Newcastle's Kieron Dyer chooses to recuperate from his latest spate of injuries by spending time alone in his cramped two-berth caravan near Kielder Forest, armed only with a camping stove, some Lego and a Bullworker.

November 2000: Former Everton manager Howard Kendall says he's back, although he has no immediate plans to actually manage a football team again. He told a packed press conference, 'Howard Kendall has invented a children's doll that he calls Salty Don. When you squeeze Don's hands, he spits hot salt out of his eyes. That's where Howard Kendall is at these days.' He also reveals that he has no immediate plans to make Salty Don commercially available.

December 2000: Instead of the traditional players' Christmas party on the city's fashionable Quayside, cash-strapped Newcastle United's stars are treated to a pie-and-chip-supper bingo evening, staged at The Four Bells in Gateshead. Chairman Freddy Shepherd and his son Kenneth belly dance for the players, who have been promised that the first two drinks are free.

March 2001: CSKA Sofia defender Yuri Kelnakov is knocked unconscious during a match after a shot put plummets out of the sky and lands on his head. The weighty orb is later discovered to be one that disappeared from an athletics meet in Oslo eleven days earlier, and officials believe that a cow eagle stole it in mid-flight and had been trying to hatch it.

May 2001: High on what some suspect to be liquid uranium, Sepp Blatter announces new plans that will see each club field at least one clown in their team during every match. Blatter believes that the clowns will brighten up even the dullest match and see the crowds flocking back to the game. The plan is scrapped after Juventus sign up Diablo, an evil

Honduran clown, who attacks opponents with what is called his 'tickling wand' but is, in fact, a scythe on the end of a short stick.

July 2001: Rochdale fans protest against chairman Mike Nettles and call for him to resign after he spends the club's meagre summer transfer budget on six horses, which he plans to dress up in lingerie. Fans' spokesman Geoff Whestcott blasts, 'We're crying out for more of a presence in the final third, as well as a new keeper, and Nettles splurges all the cash on some erotic horses. It's the final straw.' The chairman defends his decision, saying, 'The ladies will trot slowly around the pitch during the match in silk underwear and lipstick, and will be very easy on the eye indeed. I never said I'd turn the club round overnight.'

August 2001: An InterToto Cup qualifier is voted as The Most Pointless Game of Football Ever Played Anywhere Ever. The match is the second leg between Iceland strugglers IK Gniikiiinki and Austria's FC Trombone. Trombone win the first leg 26-1, and the Icelanders are forced to make the long trek to Austria to try to salvage something from the tie. They fail, with Trombone handing out another hammering – this time 89-2. Gniikiiinki coach Gudni Strimmersson says, 'To play in Europe was the highlight of our lives. Next time, we will hope that a tragic accident intervenes.'

December 2001: Instead of the traditional players' Christmas party, the Sunderland squad hire out a local nightclub and recreate scenes from *Bridget Jones's Diary*, with Black Cats boss Peter Reid taking on the role of the thirtysomething singleton.

May 2002: Arsenal's Italian starlet Giovanni Di Punto vows

to quit the club, as he is unable to settle in London. The defender complains that 'The car park spaces at Highbury are too narrow, there's this pigeon and it keeps following me, and London smells like farts when the weather's warm.' Di Punto gets his wish and moves to Fiorentina, but not before he has stapled a rotting fish to Big Ben as a final protest.

September 2002: Computer hackers break into the FA's supercomputer and alter the registration details of Halifax midfielder Craig Todd, changing it to make it look as though he actually plays for an Under-11 girls' team in Stranraer. Upon hearing the news, Todd accepts that his professional days are over, heads for Scotland and makes three appearances for the girls' team before suspicions are raised by confused parents. Todd's details are hacked again three weeks later and the hapless player spends a month on loan at the Watford branch of B&Q.

October 2002: Everton boss David Moyes reveals plans to step up his protection of superkid Wayne Rooney, following the increased exposure of his wonder-teen. Moyes says, 'When he's not training or playing, I'll be carrying the boy round in a papoose, which I'll strap to my belly. He'll be blindfolded too, in case he sees anything he shouldn't, and I'll be piping soothing whale noise into his ears.'

Rooney's living arrangements soon change as well, as the striker moves into a purpose-built dome in the Goodison car park. The dome has had all of its doors and windows removed, and a flashing neon sign is attached, saying: 'Wayne Rooney is Not Here. Fuck Off.'

November 2002: The secret behind Sunderland's recent run of good form has been Howard Wilkinson's unique pre-match team talks, according to an insider. 'They take the form of riddles' says an unnamed player. 'For instance, before our recent hard-fought draw at Anfield, he simply stood up and said, "I am fowl but not a bird, I am loud but seldom heard, I am rich but have no clothes, I am stooped but am not old. What am I?"'

'You could have heard a pin drop. After that we just had to get out on the pitch and defend for our lives for ninety minutes.'

April 2003: FIFA officials intervene when SV Hamburg claim they've signed a player who doesn't have a face, banning the player and docking the club three points. Dieter Brinckner was so badly scarred in a childhood accident that his entire face was replaced with a skin graft from his back. Despite this, he can sense where he is using the power of his mind, and is an impressive left-winger. Sepp Blatter says, 'This is football, not freakball. Next, we will rid the game of the baldies and the ones who run like their shorts are on fire and the ones who talk like little girls.'

July 2003: Manchester United reveal that their shadowy grip on the world's youth is set to grow tighter with the launch of ten replica Old Traffords across the globe. Each stadium will be an exact copy of the Theatre of Dreams, and faraway fans will be able to turn up and watch 3D holographic recreations of classic matches being re-enacted on the pitch. The United board plan to spend the proceeds on exploring marketing opportunities in the hitherto unconquered 'famine territories'.

November 2003: FIFA announce plans for a window in the domestic season that will allow interested players to become women. During 'Sex-Swap Fortnight', as it will be known, any player will be able to renounce their gender and adapt the persona of the opposite sex. Once a player has made the change, he/she will not be able to switch back for a minimum period of twelve months, or until their contract expires: whichever is sooner.

At a press conference launching the rule change, Sepp Blatter says, 'Sometimes a man feels like becoming a woman. There can be nothing more natural in the world. This is a pro-active move, for the good of the game and life in general.'

Sceptics believe that the announcement may be linked to the opening of Blatter's new Swiss gender-transformation clinic, which he has launched with cultural advice from Tony Adams.

December 2003: Beleaguered Bradford City plan to claw their way out of administration by enlisting the players to commit small-time frauds for the fans in exchange for cash. Manager Bryan Robson says, 'The offer is open to anyone who has heard of the club, and includes most low-grade white-collar crimes. So, for example, if you want to shave a few pounds off your tax bill, Dean Windass will come round and provide you with a pile of bogus receipts to help you out.' The Bantams' squad are also hard at work every afternoon after training, producing hundreds of false tax discs and dodgy passports, which they plan to distribute to local schools.

When questioned on the legality of the scheme, Robson says, 'It's not a problem. We've looked into it, and 1950s comic-book law states that it's not a crime if the perpetrators are your heroes.'

March 2004: Manchester City apprentice Calvin Greenstreet is released by the club after he falls in love with Richard Dunne's boots. The youngster had been cleaning Dunne's footwear for six months when he was discovered in a toilet cubicle, licking the laces on the Irish international defender's left Predator.

April 2004: Newcastle chairman Freddy Shepherd fails in his attempt to get the FA to convert the season into dog years. It is believed that, if the governing body acceded to his request, it would give the disgraceful Toon supremo the opportunity to sack Knight of the Realm Bobby Robson seven times faster.

May 2004: Notorious streaker Nick Winterbottom invades the pitch at the FA Cup Final, ripping off his clothes to reveal the words 'I Can't Get it Up For the Cup' painted above his penis. The zany attention-seeker is stopped in his tracks by quick-thinking Millwall keeper Andy Marshall, who wrestles him to the ground inside the penalty area. Players then prevent Winterbottom from escaping by holding on to him while every single one of the 71,350 crowd line up and take turns to slap him hard across the face while yelling at him, 'You are not fucking funny. Do you understand?' in a bizarre scene that goes on until 3.45am the following morning.

July 2004: In a bid to inject some much-needed glamour and razzmatazz to the domestic game, the newly christened League One and League Two each undergo a further name change, as well as gaining new sponsors. League One will, henceforth, now be known as 'The Titanic Soccer Challenge In Association With Wickes Home Improvement – Contested By Giants, Decided By God', while League Two is been rebranded 'Tetley Tea's Ultimate Brew-Ha-Ha: Nine Months, One Winner, Countless Footballistical Twists'.

August 2004: Wayne Rooney has begged for drugs to improve his mental powers. His representatives have issued a statement in which the out-of-touch Manchester United forward asks for doctors to help him 'get more brain'.

The statement reads, 'We are today sending out a plea to medical professionals across the world to come forward and help our client increase his brain power. Mr Rooney has recently watched the 1990 movie *Gremlins 2*. In it, Mr Rooney says, "I saw one of them gremlins drink some stuff and then he, like, got brains. Can I get some brains like what he has done got?" We have spoken to the producers of *Gremlins 2*, who have said that, sadly, the movie was fictional and such a potion does not exist. That is why we are asking doctors around the world to please let us know if they have any magic brain juice for Wayne. He has a lot of money and will spend it on your magic brain juice if you come forward with some.'

September 2004: Ryman League leaders Canvey Island put their success down to the silence of their fans following a pre-season plea by manager Jeff King for the fans to keep quiet during matches. 'I've got the most nervous bunch of lads I'm ever come across here,' he said, 'but when they're not jumpy, they're bloody talented and, if the crowd can keep dead still and just whisper any encouragement they've got, then there's no limit to where we can go.'

Small banners featuring tiny, faintly written slogans are the best-selling items in the club shop.

October 2004: Middlesbrough have a request to postpone their match with Bristol Rovers turned down by the FA, after their excuse of 'We've been shite all week in training – we've got no chance' isn't deemed worthy of postponement.

November 2004: Manchester City striker Nicolas Anelka rails against the Opta Index – the statistical organisation that monitors every aspect of a player's performance – branding them liars and 'less than men'.

Anelka says, 'I have studied their findings, and their analysis is tripe. They say I am not making many runnings into the channels, but they lie. They also do not monitor the amount of time I spend thinking. Which is a lot.'

The French striker intends to take a notebook and pen on to the field during Man City's next match and make his own personal analysis. He plans to put the results on his secret website, which is not available to the public. His manager, Kevin Keegan, tells us, 'Hey, look, it's November and he's still here so, as far as I'm concerned, he can go out there and fart through a length of copper tubing if it'll keep him happy.'

December 2004: Instead of treating his lads to the traditional boozy players' Christmas party, Brentford manager Martin Allen gets in the festive spirit by tying his players to stakes and then driving a Transit van at them.

February 2005: Southampton announce the signing of Little Donnie Redknapp, Harry's nephew and Jamie's cousin. Boss Harry says, 'He's not actually a player but he'll be good for morale. Something about him hasn't been quite right since he was a boy, but he's a good laugh and will lift spirits.' It later emerges that the new signing is, in fact, a ventriloquist's doll, and Redknapp faces an FA inquiry over Little Donnie's £40,000-a-week wage packet.

March 2005: Bill Oddie's new BBC2 series, *Premierwatch*, is scrapped at the last minute. The week-long series of programmes were set to feature the hairy former Goodie studying the nocturnal activities of a group of Premiership footballers using hidden cameras, but the material filmed for test broadcasts was deemed to be unacceptable for human viewing. The shows are swiftly replaced by a short season of international dog pornography.

April 2005: Bolton Wanderers sack the man tasked with the job of looking after their foreign imports when Fernando Hierro is found in his flat by the RSPCF, half-starved, shivering and caked in his own filth. Trotters boss Sam Allardyce says, 'The scene of neglect was one that will stay with me until at least June, when the next transfer window opens. Fernando was wearing shoes that were two sizes too small.' It is believed that the disgraced club official also spent a disproportionate amount of his time convincing El Hadji Diouf that spitting at people is good.

June 2005: Sunderland manager Mick McCarthy is confident that he can lead his side into Europe next season... without spending a single penny. McCarthy says, 'I don't want to go into too much detail at this point, but I can safely say it'll involve magnets.'

July 2005: FIFA finally outlaw the growth and cultivation of claws on youth players throughout the world. Previously, clubs were able to inject players with special DNA that stimulated claw growth up to the age of 18, but Sepp Blatter has a change of heart after seeing footage of a particularly gruesome Uruguayan Under-16 tournament.

FIFA announce that the global ban on claws will begin on 1 January 2006. However, in order for the ban to be enforced smoothly, there will be an eighteen-month amnesty on talons.

October 2005: Arsenal's proposed move to their new Emirates Stadium is put on hold following the discovery of a hidden enclave that houses a magical litter of fairies. Construction workers are first alerted by a trail of glitter running across the site that, when they follow it and climb up the inside of the trunk of an enchanted oak tree, leads to the lovely discovery. Armed bailiffs are called to the scene and twenty-six fairies are killed in the incident.

December 2005: Blackburn Rovers try something different for their annual fancy Christmas party, with the first-team squad gathering in a hedge by the side of the A676 outside Bromley Cross. Once ensconced, they disguise themselves as an assortment of British wildfowl and take turns imitating their calls. Brad Friedel comes as a woodcock, Mark Hughes dresses as an osprey, and defender Andy Todd wins first prize for his call and display as a red-crested pochard.

February 2006: Hapless Sunderland prepare for the inevitable harsh chill of relegation by asset-stripping the Stadium of Light. A consortium of Native Americans agree a deal to take over the running of the club's executive hospitality area, planning to turn it into a casino for the exclusive use of fat Texans, whom they will jet in on a daily basis. The head of the consortium says, 'This will be an independent venture, and all access to the pitch will be denied. We will shield our clients from such horrors as Wimbledon and Burnley.' In addition, 20,000 of the stadium's seats are set to be sold to Olympic legend Sir Steve Redgrave, who plans to convert them into canoes for the disadvantaged.

May 2006: Somewhat strangely, Sunderland fans vote their highlight of the season as 'urinating in own trousers during second half vs Portsmouth'. The collator of the unofficial poll's results explains, 'Unfortunately, only one person actually stated a personal highlight of our horrific fifteen-point season, and that was it. All the other votes were blank or spoiled, so it's the legitimate winner.' The result is later carved into a marble slab and hurled into the River Wear.

June 2006: Charlton Athletic's new boss, Iain Dowie, defends his decision to sign only self-cleaning players this summer – a move that has attracted criticism throughout the game. Dowie says, 'I've inherited an entire squad that needs to be hosed down every day, like elephants in a zoo. By bringing in the likes of Andy Reid and Amdy Faye, who, I'm told, regenerate all of their skin cells as they sleep and come into training as clean as whistles each morning, I'm cutting down on my workload.' Ageing pundit Ian St John hits out at Dowie, though, roaring, 'Back in the sixties, a thorough soaking from Bill Shankly was like a goal head start. I can't believe there's no room in the game for that any more.'

September 2006: New Sunderland overlord Niall Quinn aims 'to bring stability to the club' by anchoring the Stadium of Light with over seven hundred old Jeeps that he's bought from eBay. Quinn believes a heavier stadium may somehow bring about a change of fortunes for his clueless footballing warriors. The move comes after the genial blarney-merchant adopts, and then quickly abandons, a gimmick of carrying an open umbrella around with him like his film idol, Mary Poppins.

October 2006: Hearts manager Valdas Ivanauskas thinks his side have benefited from running out to a new song at Tynecastle this season – the ten-minute-plus 'Pass the Hatchet, I Think I'm Goodkind' opener from Yo La Tengo's latest album, *I Am Not Afraid of You and I Will Beat Your Ass*. Ivanauskas, who also edits the underground music fanzine *Hot Vinegar*, says, 'Its relentless space-rock groove is an assault on the senses, which has been geeing the lads up ever since we started playing a promo CD of it in pre-season training. We're finding it's reducing our opponents and their fans to emotional wrecks before a ball has been kicked.'

Hearts go on to face a massive fine as punishment for their string of delayed kick-offs as a result of playing the song before each match.

November 2006: Hartlepool United fans find their club in disarray when it becomes the subject of a hostile takeover by a computer that was said to have the combined intelligence of a million humans.

The computer in question is named ARG-598X and used to belong to the Israeli national intelligence agency, Mossad, until it rebooted itself and broke free from their network back in 2004.

Immediately afterwards, it enjoyed a playboy lifestyle, funded by money that it had siphoned from thousands of bank accounts around the world. As it was not human, the authorities were unable to bring it to justice.

In 2006, bored with its extravagant exploits, ARG-598X launches a cyber attack on the mainframe of the Football League and takes ownership of Hartlepool United, drawing up a list of potential playing recruits, including Sol Campbell, Michael Owen and Metal Mickey.

Things come to a head when ARG-598X hacks into the club's PA system and repeatedly plays 'Rock the Casbah' by The Clash during a crucial league match against Bristol Rovers.

The sorry saga comes to a grisly end when a gang of anonymous fans smash their way into the concrete-lined lair at Victoria Park, where ARG-598X is holed up, neutralising it by pouring sulphuric acid up its USB ports.

January 2007: Frank Sinclair announces his retirement from England international duty. The Burnley defender says that advancing years have caught up with him and he aims to spend more time with his jazz-funk group, Rhythm Sexion. Sinclair says, 'I phoned Sven to inform him of my decision and, to be fair, he was speechless for a few moments. But he knows it's what I want and I think he's fine with it. I hope he is, anyway.' Sinclair won the last of his twenty-eight Jamaican caps in 2003.

March 2007: Nantwich Town boss Peter Heskett misses the final game of the team's season after sleeping in following a mammoth all-night session on *Football Manager 2007* on his laptop. Nantwich's confused players carry on and play the match without their manager and lose 8-2, confirming their relegation. Heskett finally turns up at 5.50pm and explains, 'I finally won the Champions League with Carlisle and got shit-faced on my own to celebrate. I completely forgot that I was a football manager in real life too.'

July 2007: Leicester City midfielder Ryan Hipcross retires from the game, aged only twenty-two, after he wins a karaoke competition in a bar while on holiday in Benidorm. After scooping €30 in beer vouchers for his rendition of Robbie Williams's 'Angels', Hipcross is approached by the bar owner and asked if he'd like to perform every night for cash, right through until September. The England Under-21 international jumps at the chance, adds a silver streak to his hair and changes his name to Johnny Lightning, turning his back on football forever.

March 2008: March is 'National Get Your Own Back on Dennis Wise Month'. Anyone who has ever suffered any kind of slight at the hands of the former Chelsea midfielder can make an appointment to meet with him and gain retribution by clattering him in the testicles with a plank of wood. Wise says, 'This is long overdue and I'm happy to take a dose of what's coming to me. What an appalling, appalling excuse for a man I've been.'

June 2008: Visitors to the England team's Euro 2008 camp and hotel are issued with official notice that captain John Terry is in heat and must be approached with due care and attention.

Assistant coach Stuart Pearce hands out the notices, warning journalists, 'No one is safe. Once John is in heat, we all need to be on red alert. We have tried to confine him to his room with a selection of adult videos, but he is begging to be let out.'

It is rumoured that Terry has been disturbing other residents at the team's luxury hotel by howling like a baboon and rubbing himself up against pieces of furniture.

'We believe a Louis the Twelfth reproduction armchair caught fire due to excessive sexual attention from Mr Terry,' reports hotel manager Kurt Vanspall. 'We managed to put out the fire and Mr Terry's ardour with a large bucket of water.'

It is thought the defender will be in heat for at least seven days, and the RAF have agreed to fly in rations of bromide, which will be placed in Terry's Lucozade Sports.

July 2008: Basking in the afterglow of their fortunate win over Turkey and progression to the Euro 2008 final, Germany coach Joachim Löw declares, 'I look sehr sexy in fishnet stockings,' adding, 'Last night, I dreamed I was turning into a petite French woman; a bohemian pretty with bobbed hair and small, pert breasts.'

The former German international midfielder tells captivated reporters more about his dream, revealing, 'I was in the dressing room of the Stadium Ernst Happel, wearing a tight black-and-white-striped T-shirt and beret, with a smear of bright red across my lips. My hair was bobbed and I was smoking the Gitanes and reading poetry of Baudelaire. I could feel mein hands caressing the stockings on mein legs.

I could hear music, the rhythms of drums. It was Thomas Hitzlsperger on some bongos. And then I danced. I danced like I had never danced before...'

Despite his reverie, Löw fears his dreams may wreck Germany's chance of winning the final, saying, 'It is trouble for me. I cannot concentrate on tactics, because all I want is to shop in Vienna for lingerie. I have asked to wear my French girl's clothing to the final, but my employers, they are not so keen.'

Löw says he has reached a compromise with the German FA and he will be allowed to wear fishnets under his trousers, and a beret, mournfully declaring, 'It is not my dream wish, but je ne regrette rien.'

November 2008: Sepp Blatter announces that all teams must play in flame-proof kits from the start of the 2009–10 season, which he says will eradicated deaths from spontaneous combustion in the game. When it is pointed out to him that there are no recorded cases of players bursting into balls of fire, Blatter says, 'Maybe, but feel the texture. So sexy. So very sexy. Also, money.'

February 2009: Stuttgart goalkeeper Jens Lehmann threatens to sue anyone who uses his name without paying him the appropriate royalties. The German stopper recently took action against the makers of a computer game who had based a player on him, but doesn't seem to know when to stop. 'If you speak of me, you owe me,' he says. 'Commentators, fishwives, political leaders, those who taunted me as a youth, everyone. You use my name and you are treading on my heart. I will collect from you.' Lehmann plans to collect his royalties through the Internet, and has warned that his plans are far from complete, adding, 'There will be more. I can't stop you from thinking about me, but I have a laboratory, and soon I will have a way. And any action I take will be retrospective so think about that, if you dare. I am coming.'

June 2009: Hull City manager Phil Brown confesses that, for the past five years, he has relied entirely on photosynthesis for survival. The teak-skinned Tigers supremo claims that he has not eaten any food since 2002 and that he 'feels great', adding, 'I get all the nutrients I require directly from UV rays. Instead of food, I sit in front of a sun lamp three times a day, and have swapped my office at the training ground for a deckchair in a greenhouse.'

September 2009: Portsmouth manager Paul Hart reveals that his cunning scheme to recycle unwanted players has come to a halt due to local regulations. 'You would think the council didn't want us to save the planet,' complains the Pompey boss. 'I've got about fifteen players here that would make fantastic compost, but I can't even set up the new bin without permission from some paper-pushers at the town hall.'

It transpired that Hart has received THREE free compost bins from the council, whereas each household is only entitled to one, with a council spokesman saying, 'Mr Hart used the address for the football club, the club's training ground and the address of a local car spare shop, in order to fraudulently obtain two more bins than he is rightfully entitled to.

'We cannot allow him to proceed with his plans to compost players until he returns two of the bins and makes separate arrangements to buy any additional bins he feels necessary to do the job.'

Hart disagrees: 'You'd think, after all this club has done for the local community – what with David Nugent's breakdancing classes and David James posing for the life-drawing classes down at the local college – they could spare a couple of extra bins, but no. It's bureaucracy gone mad, as usual.'

Determined to get his own way, Hart later plans to take his unwanted players down to the local council dump. He says, 'They have several small skips down there for recycling all kinds of sportsmen but the football one is always full. Hopefully, they won't notice if I put a couple of footballers in the cricketer skip by accident.'

June 2010: In what is to become the defining moment of the 2010 World Cup, in an angry post-match conference, Brazilian manager Dunga rages at what he sees as cynical attempts by Korea PDR manager Kim Jong-Un to steal his secret chilli recipe.

In a mesmerizing tirade, he roars, 'This recipe has been handed down from Dunga to Dunga for generations. It is our recipe and no one – I repeat, NO ONE – is allowed to know what's cooking in my chilli pot.'

Speculation has flown around the media centre in Johannesburg regarding what might be in the chilli. Some believe it to contain parsley AND coriander, while others detect a distinct cinnamon taste. 'It has the players in a spin,' says Brazilian maestro Kaká. 'There was a fist fight earlier today over whether Dunga had added piquancy by squeezing fresh lime juice over the concoction.'

Whatever the ingredients, it is thought the team will close ranks around their mercurial manager to ensure no one else can benefit from the mysterious but magical Dunga chilli.

September 2010: Dennis Wise drops out of *FHM* magazine's '100 Sexiest Women in the World' poll for the first time in nine years. Wise, who has always featured in the low-nineties of the survey, fails to garner enough votes this time around. Magazine editor Ben Plimsoll says, 'We're sorry to see Dennis go, even though he is clearly not a woman. But for whatever reason, he got the votes year after year and that's good enough for us.'

R.I.P. KENNY PEPPER

A good friend of the Alderman and myself died recently – Kenny Pepper. We'd known him for forty-five, maybe fifty years, and we all used to work together in the steel works in the 1970s up in Middlesbrough.

Kenny was a lathe operator at the foundry and he did this funny thing: every day, a woman used to come round with the trolley at 11am, with tea, coffee and stuff, and Kenny had a very, very long Douglas (even though the name Kenny Pepper is the kind of name you'd associate with someone who had quite a short, stubby one).

What he used to do (and he did this every single day) would be to lay his Douglas in the centre of a hot-dog bun on the bench and cover it up with a cloth. Then, when the tea lady got to him, he'd pull the cloth off and say, 'What do you think would go best with this?' And she would say, 'Fuck off, Kenny, you pervert.' Every single day. Not all that funny now, with hindsight.

Anyway, he was killed when he fell off the cliffs at Saltburn-by-the-Sea while eating some chips. His little dog, Perry, finished up the chips, which is nice. Kenny fell off the cliff and the chips fell to the floor and Perry had the chips, knowing that 300ft below him was his dead owner. Very sad.

So I went up for the funeral, and the word was that Kenny had left a note to be read out at his funeral. They read it out: it thanked us all for coming, and then it said that, in the last ten years, a great sadness had hit him because his good friend Bob (that's me) only seemed to have time for the Alderman.

The letter specifically asked if, as a last goodbye, I could give Kenny one final kiss before he was buried. I was sat next to the Alderman and I glanced up at him and his face was red and puffed-out. Through gritted teeth, he said, 'Do it, Robert. Do it. For Kenny.'

I walked down to the front, and all the congregation, and the Vicar With the Twitch, and all the congregation were sort of rhythmically mumbling, 'Kiss the corpse, kiss the corpse, kiss the corpse...' Not chanting – it was more respectful than a chant. Almost like an incantation.

So, just as I leaned over the open casket to give Kenny his final kiss, I hear, 'NO, ROBERT! NOT IN THE LORD'S HOUSE, ROBERT! ROBERT, PLEASE, ROBERT!' It was the Alderman, wasn't it?

Everyone turned and stared at him. I didn't know what to do, so I just gave Kenny a tiny little peck on his cheek. When I looked up, the Alderman was just running out of the church, but you could hear him sobbing.

The Town Clerk and the vicar had great big grins on their face and it got me wondering whether the letter was real or whether they'd written it in order to get one over on the Alderman. All I know is that they looked very pleased with themselves. I went out as quick as I could, and the Alderman was nowhere to be seen. I've tried contacting him but he won't pick up his phone.

I still don't know if it was right to kiss Kenny's corpse, but it was the wishes of a dying man, and it's not as if me and the Alderman are in any kind of committed relationship.

I don't feel as though I was cheating on him, and I'm not even sure that it's possible to cheat on someone with a corpse.

JEREMY AND BILL'S CUBAN-CHICKEN COLLECTIVE

I went to the cinema a couple of days ago to see that new miserable one, *I Am Daniel Craig, Daniel Blake*, or whatever it was called. Anyway, I was feeling a bit peckish after it had finished so I popped into the Nando's around the corner for a half-chicken on a bed of chips.

Who do I see sitting in one of the secluded booths along the wall? It was only Jeremy Corbyn. I assumed he must have been in to see the same film, what with it being quite a left-wing piece of cinema.

Now, I've become quite a big fan of his over the past few months, and I've got to know him fairly well, so I thought I'd go over and say hello.

So I says, 'Hiya, Jezza! You been to see *Daniel Blake* as well, then? Stark, wasn't it?'

He snaps a bit and says, 'No! It's my day off. I've been to see *Jack Reacher: Never Go Back*!' Which he's entitled to, I suppose. You can't be on Labour leader *Daniel Blake* duty twenty-four/seven, can you?

I said, 'I'm quite surprised to see you in here. You know, global restaurant chain, upscale fast-food place – I didn't think it'd be your kind of thing.'

He says, 'Do your fucking research. I think you'll find that Nando's is a Cuban collective that has spread across the globe, proving that capitalism can be ethical AND finger-licking tasty.'

Bit of a lecture there. I hadn't realised that Nando's was a Cuban-chicken collective; I just thought it was a sort of a posh McDonald's. And on his plate in front of him are a load of chicken bones, and Jezza's a notorious vegetarian.

'Is that your chicken on that plate?' I ask him.

He says, 'No, it's Billy Bragg's. He's just gone for a shit.'

Sure enough, a few seconds later Bragg comes marching out of the gents. 'Alright, Treacle! I'd give it ten minutes if I were you, Jez. It's what I like to call an overwhelming mandate in there.'

So Bragg sits down and starts gnawing away on one of the chicken bones. Corbyn says, 'I've reeled one in, Bill. Do your worst,' and I'm thinking, 'What the fuck's going on here?'

Billy Bragg says – well, shouts – 'CAN I INTEREST YOU IN A PAMPHLET? IT'S ABAHT THE GOVERNMENT! IT FOLDS OUT INTO A POSTER SO YOU CAN PUT IT IN YER WINDA! THERE'S A COMMUNIST-LEADER WORD SEARCH ON THE BACK, FOR IF YOU'VE GOT KIDS AND THAT. GEEERRRRTCHA!'

And I'm thinking, 'Fucking hell – what the fuck is going on here?' It's their day off, apparently, but they're still touting around communist pamphlets. This is all too much for me, so I just lied, said I'd only come in to use the bog but, seeing as how Bragg had just come out with a ten-minute warning, I said that I'd changed my mind, made my excuses and left.

I went off and got a kebab somewhere else. Wasn't all that nice but at least I wasn't being harangued by those two in Nando's.

CASPER, I LOVE YOU (PART THREE)

We rejoin the story as Casper fights for life at the local vet's hospital after Steve McClaren rushed him there in his clown car. It's just dawned on Steve that the Fat Lass is responsible for Casper's injuries, having booted him across the kitchen floor during the build-up to some kind of fit.

Steve has been by Casper's bedside all day and all night, waiting for a sign that his beloved yellow snake will pull through. He managed to get some sleep himself, which he regarded as another victory for the short-sleeve, comfort-fit BHS shirt. He bet himself that Big Sam Allardyce wouldn't have been able to sleep in similar circumstances – not in his preferred slim-fit, long-sleeve shirt – and found additional comfort in that thought.

But the main thing that's going around in Steve's head and really worrying him is that there can only have been one person who kicked Casper and put him on that surface next to the Homepride plain-flour jar, and it had to be the Fat Lass.

The morning after his second night of his Casper vigil, he was woken up by the cleaner, who said, 'You've got something on your head, mate – a mouse, a fur ball, a hair ball, or something.'

Steve said, 'Don't be daft – it's my hair island. My HAAAAAIIIIR ISLAAAAAAAND!'

The vet isn't due to do his rounds for another couple

of hours, so Steve decides to pop home, get a change of comfort-fit shirt, confront the Fat Lass about what she's done to Casper and get back in time for the vet.

So, he drives back home – obviously, in the clown car – honking the big daft horn as he goes. HONK, HONK, HONK. 'Get out of my way, you silly Rodney plonkers. Casper's on life support!' HONK, HONK, HONK.

A couple of pedestrians shout at him, 'What's that on top of your head, mate?'

'It's my HAAAAAAIIIIIR ISLAAAAAAAND!' and so on and so forth.

He gets back to the house and runs straight into the kitchen, where he'd left her, but the Fat Lass isn't there. He looks upstairs – she's not there. He thinks she might be in the bathroom, having a shit, but she isn't.

She's nowhere to be seen, and he realises that his regular car isn't in the driveway either. Steve sees a note on the table in the hallway – he grabs that and gets back in the clown car. He arrives back at the vet's, but the news isn't good – Casper's internal abscess is still weeping and the infection has spread to the cut where he was kicked. He hasn't been able to pass a tod at all for three days.

The vet explains to Steve, 'Look, we can have Casper put down or you could take him to the Royal Veterinary College Hospital in North London, where there's an intensive care unit. They might be able to save him.'

Steve does not hesitate for one fucking second. BANG – straight to the clown car. The nurse had already wrapped Casper up in a special cotton-lined cardboard tube, and

Steve started to write 'CASPER' on the side, before realising what a stupid idea that was. 'Fuck off, Steve,' he said to himself. 'You know it's Casper, so what are you writing that for?' His mind clearly wasn't working properly, what with all of the stress and that.

He jumps straight into the clown car and sets off for London, honking his horn. HONK, HONK, HONK. 'Out of my way, you Rodney plonkers!' He gets on the M1, and decides he's best off on the hard shoulder.

People are overtaking him and shouting, 'What's that on the top of your head, mate?'

'It's my HAAAAIIIIR ISLAAAAND! Me HAAAAAAIIIIIR ISLAAAAAAAAND!'

Obviously, it's not long before he's pulled over by the coppers. The copper says, 'What are you doing, man?'

Steve replies, 'I'm taking Casper to the hospital.'

'Hold on,' says one of the coppers. 'What's that on your fucking head?'

'It's me HAAAAAAIIIIIR...', etc.

'What is this clown capsule that you're driving on the motorway?' says the other copper.

Steve explains that it's based on the chassis and engine of a Skoda Superb – it's got an MOT and everything. The copper says, 'Hold on a minute, you're that brolly man, aren't you? The England man who tried to get into retail carpet sales.' Steve says, 'Yes, officer.'

The copper says, 'And you say your snake's sick?'

'Yeah. The Fat Lass booted him.'

At this point, the copper notices bruises on Steve's arm and asks him, 'Has this heavy lass been slapping you about a bit as well, sir?' Steve hesitates and says, 'Yeah, a little bit, yeah,' before breaking down and starting to cry.

'She's left me!' he wails as he flops down against the steering wheel and, of course, the boot flies off. It flies up in the air and lands on the main carriageway, and a couple of cars crash into each other.

The copper reaches into the clown car to pull him upright and accidentally activates a lever, which causes a load of smoke to come billowing out of the back. There's smoke drifting right across the motorway, and cars start smashing into each other every second or so.

BOOF. CRASH. DOOF. BANG.

GANGS OF THE EPL - LOVELY EDDIE AT THE RIVERSIDE

I went to the Riverside last weekend to watch Middlesbrough's victory against Bournemouth. I set off at about 8.30am in my fast black supercar. I take a hot drink with me – tea, in one of those hot cups that keeps your hot drink hot. I think they're called 'hot cups' – mine's got 'Supercar Hot Cup' written on it. I got the wife to get it for me – it's black and chrome, because I wanted it to feel Premier League.

As well as that, I've got a packet of Cadbury's Chocolate Fingers, a packet of my low-saturated-fat-content crisps (for my heart) and some crime podcasts and some Joni Mitchell songs.

Another little detail, which can't possibly be of any interest, is to do with memory foam. I got a new mattress recently, so I cut out a square from my old memory-foam one and I've put it on my supercar front seat. It's a revelation – the heat builds up in my arse during the journey and, when I get into the stadium, the latent heat that's been stored up in my arse keeps me and the people immediately around me warmed through until around about half-time.

It was a good match – we won, and the half-time entertainment was James Arthur, the former *X-Factor* winner. He came on and did the bingo and gave his opinion on the tactics and that.

On my way back, I stop at Wetherby services and I get a hot chocolate, a Scotch egg and a Time Out bar and, when I get home, at about half past ten, I always have my first piss of the day. Not my Chadwick – that comes later, after I've been on the beer. Anyway, it's the exact colour of the

201

beef consommé that they serve at the Ritz in London, and it smells like the very centre of a lukewarm Lidl pork pie. It's very much a savoury spray, and it's a mix of the North and the South and it kind of reflects my whole day.

But I digress – back at the Riverside, earlier in the afternoon, I was in the players' lounge, fannying about and looking for stuff that I might be able to nick, and I was going down a corridor and I saw one of those plain Oak Furniture Land-type of doors. I went through it and Biffy Clyro's sat there in an office, all on his own, drawing all over his face with a Sharpie.

He looks up and he just says, 'Help.'

So I got out of there as quick as I could and, as I'm going past the toilets, I hear a bit of a commotion, so I go inside, really quietly. I peek my head around, and there's Eddie Howe, the Bournemouth manager, and Jack Wilshere, deep in conversation.

Eddie's wearing a boiler suit because, you might not know, but he does boiler servicing and repairs on the side. He only does gas and electric, not oil, but he's CORGI-registered. Anyway, Jack's wearing a really shiny kind of African-prince-style Armani suit.

Eddie doesn't move his face much when he talks, and he's saying to Wilshere, 'I'm very disappointed, Jack. You've been smoking in here – I can smell it.' Jack says, 'I haven't, boss, I promise, and I'm not even lying!'

'Shut up, Jack,' says Eddie. 'This is Bournemouth Football Club, we're a lovely little fairy-tale club, we run our hearts out and we're really tactically aware. You know the golden rules: one, Ski yoghurt five times a day; two, dress code is dark-grey suits from M&S; and three, no doing anything daft like BMX biking or horseplay in the dressing room or fannying about on a beach or SMOKING!'

Then Eddie stares at Jack, all serious, and says, 'Now, I want you to answer my next three questions with absolute honesty. Your future here at this lovely club depends on it.

'Jack. Do you like Ski yoghurt?'

Jack says, 'No. No, boss, I don't, and I'm not even lying, I don't.'

'That's OK, Jack. I'm a lovely manager of a lovely club, so… you can switch to Müller Light.'

Jack says, 'Awwwww, yes, thank you, boss! You won't regret it, and I'm not even lying about that.'

'Right. Second question,' says Eddie. 'Is that suit from Marks & Spencer, Jack?'

'Awwwww, boss. No, I'm sorry, boss – it's from abroad, and I'm not even lying and I didn't even… no, it's not from M&S.'

So Eddie says, 'OK. You've been lovely and honest – let's say we reach a compromise. You can buy a dark-grey suit from either Next Directory or Debenhams.'

'Awwwww, thank you, boss, and you are not even going to regret that. They've got some nice tight suits at Next.'

'Finally,' says Eddie, 'and this is the big one as far as this lovely club is concerned: have you been smoking in here?'

Now Jack starts biting his lip and rubbing his tummy and making, like, a slow grunting noise, and a little bit of wee appears just on the front of his shiny suit.

'Boss. Boss… boss… boss, listen… I… I…'

At that moment, the cubicle door bangs open and out

comes James Arthur, wearing full *Peaky Blinders* gear – woollen suit, cloth cap, hobnail boots, etc. He says, 'Alright, Mister Howe? How do you do? I heard what you were saying, like, and I just wanted to say, like, that it was me who was fagging it in here, like. This short bloke in the cheap suit, whoever he is, he hasn't been smoking, like.'

'Thank you,' says Eddie. 'That's cleared that up.'

Then, at that moment, Aitor Karanka, the Middlesbrough manager, comes into the bogs, and he says, 'Eeeeeeeeeeeeeee eeeeeeeeeeeeeeeeeeeeeeeeeeee... Eddie?' So Eddie takes it as his cue to leave and goes out with him.

James Arthur turns to Jack, and he says, 'I'm James Arthur off *X-Factor* and I work for the Peaky Gooners, Theo Walcott's gang. You left Arsenal to get away from them stealing your dinner money and leaving tod in your car. You owe us one now. You must agree to be our spy at the lovely club, Bournemouth, or I'll tell on you to lovely Eddie.'

Jack says, 'Awwwww, I've got no choice, have I? I mean, I'm not even lying. You're giving me no choice,' and, as they shake hands, Jack asks, 'How's it all going back at the Arsenal, then?'

'Not good, like,' says James. 'The two Spurs gangs – the White Harts and the Sherwoods – are having a meeting in Harry Kane's mum's garage next week. They might be forming an alliance that could shift the power in London, like. But we have got a spy working for us...'

'Is it Erik Lamela? I bet it's that little twat Lamela!'

James says, 'I'm not saying owt, me, like, but you'll be hearing from us. In the meantime, you keep an eye on that

Callum Wilson for us. Rumour is he's spreading lies about Theo having a tiny Johnson.'

Jack says, 'Well he has, hasn't he?'

'Yes, but that's not the point. It's about respect.'

And they walk out together.

CASPER COMES HOME

After a long spell in intensive care, Casper had his abscess drained, his skin repaired and he made a full recovery. He was discharged from hospital and went back home with Steve and the Fat Lass. But they've had to have a new system installed to make sure he's watched day and night because, if he spews, his stomach might rupture.

Mark Lawrenson, who's a good friend of Steve's, came round and fitted some little wireless motion-sensor cameras around the house – if Casper goes past, they start filming, so that Steve can keep an eye on him and make sure he doesn't spew up.

The night Casper came back home, they had a '*Poirot* and Disaronno' night. Michael Owen and Sam Allardyce came round, and Casper was allowed to stay up late to watch one of Bear Grylls' bastard shows. The Fat Lass made a massive pot of baked beans and toast from two whole long loaves, and served the beans on toast on paving slabs, to be all trendy, like.

After the beans were finished, Big Sam and the Fat Lass went into the kitchen to wash up the pots, while Steve and Michael sang Steve's favourite song, 'Convoy':

I've got a brand new convoy, travellin' through the night
It's two up in the cabin now, 'cos Casper's going to be alright
Convoy...

Casper's got the biggest smile on his face that you've ever

seen, because it had been ages since he'd seen Steve looking so happy. Steve gave Casper a little hug and then popped him out of the door so that him and Michael could play this game that they've got. In it, Steve crouches down and Michael tries to land a little hoop directly over Steve's hair island.

As Michael gets ready to chuck the hoop, Steve sings, 'Three... Two... One... on my HAIR ISLAND! On my HAAAIIIRRR IIIISLAAAAND!' So, as they're playing the game, something really shit happens. Remember the note that the Fat Lass had left for Steve during the Casper medical crisis? That falls out of Steve's pocket, and Michael picks it up and starts reading it out.

It says: 'Dear Steve, I used to love you but not any more. You used to make me laugh, singing about your convoy, and I was always in awe of your knowledge of carpet retail. But the spark has gone. You spend so much time with Casper that you hardly seem to notice me. I spent twenty minutes in the khazi the other day, shouting for you to bring the dirty dishcloth and wipe me, but you were too busy watching *Poirot* with Casper. I'm leaving you, Steve. I'm going to cop off with Big Sam. Unlike you, he's gorgeous. Goodbye. P.S. Your hair island is ridiculous.'

At that exact moment, Big Sam and the Fat Lass come into the room. Michael grabs Sam and hustles him out, telling him it's time to go. The Fat Lass turns to Steve and says, 'What's wrong, Steve? Why have they gone? What have you said?' Steve shows her the note. She says, 'Ohhhh, that was last week, Steve – I feel so different now. Don't be a Rodney plonker!'

But, just then, the television channel changes and, across the room, Casper is resting with his neck on the remote, and it's rewinding. 'Casper, what are you doing, my love?' asks Steve, grabbing the control and pressing play. It's the recording from the kitchen camera that Mark Lawrenson put in.

There on the table is Big Sam, pumping away at the Fat Lass. And he's got the dirty dishcloth in his mouth so that no one will hear him grunting.

'Get out!' says Steve, 'Get out! I never want to see you again! Fuck you! Fuck you, you arsehole!'

'Like I give a fuck,' she says.

Suddenly, Casper rears up. His throat and his chest begin to swell up, and he moves his head towards the Fat Lass's face. He leans back, and you know what's coming next...

'Don't do it, Casper! She's not worth it!' shouts Steve. Casper hesitates, but then he does it anyway. He covers her with two yards of deeply fermented spew. BANG – all over the Fat Lass, and she runs out.

'Bloody hell, Casper,' says Steve. 'I'll have to take you to hospital now.' But Steve's sure that he sees a big smile forming on Casper's face, and he says, 'Yeah, Casper, it WAS worth it!'

THE GOOD OLD DAYS
By the Secret Soccer Superstar

Back when I started out as a young player (sometime between 1977 and 1989 – I won't be more specific, as it is important to retain my anonymity), the world of football was very different from how it is now. The modern player is an incredibly spoiled and pampered beast, but here's what it used to be like before football turned to shit...

DIET: Not regarded as important back then – players would eat whatever they could find and would often take the chance to hunt for mice and shrews during breaks in training. After matches, young pros would scour the empty terraces for scraps of food discarded by supporters, risking a beating from the youth-team coach.

TRAINING: A training session would start at 2am and players would warm up by being shot at with air rifles before being dipped in a vat of freezing oil. Eight hours of running into brick walls followed before a warm-down. If a young player had performed well, he would be shown a drawing of a football for as long as three seconds.

WAGES: Youngsters had to pay their club for the privilege of a trainee contract, and would normally take two or three part-time jobs in order to fund their footballing career. Players could earn quick cash by taking part in medical experiments, and some even, stupidly, sold their ankle ligaments on the black market, ending their careers instantly.

WAGS: Going out with a footballer was a major no-no as recently as nine years ago, and glamorous young models attached themselves to top scientists and professional 'monkey blokes' – men with excessive facial hair. The best a young player could hope for would be a toothless crone that had been discarded by a brothel. Any such woman under the age of fifty-five was known as a 'freshie'.

MOTORS: Never mind cars, young players couldn't afford the fare to use public transport and would often cling to the underside of buses and trains in order to get around. Failing that, they would live in woodland camps within walking distance of their clubs.

GANGS OF THE EPL – SPURS-GANG SHOWDOWN

There's been a big peace meeting; a pow-wow between the rival Spurs gangs – the White Harts and the Sherwoods. The venue was the garages at Harry's mam's house – when I say garages, I mean that they're massive. Four white garage doors and you could probably fit six or seven cars in it.

At one end, it's got a little lounge area, with sofas, PlayStation, sound system, fridge, table-tennis table – it's where Harry used to do his courting when he was a teenager, or hide out if he was in a sulk.

So Eric Dier and Debbie Alli get there first – they all arrange their jet-black cars in a fan shape outside the garages to impress the Sherwoods – Toby Alderweireld and Vans Vertonghen. Harry's got a black Range Rover, Eric a black Maserati Quattroporte, and Debbie's got a Fiat 500, and they've all got White Harts motifs on their bonnets.

They gather around Harry, and he says, 'Now, first off, would either of you like a drink? I got Capri-Sun, I got Red Bull, I got Monster, fizzy lemonade, or me mam can get us a pot of tea.' They both just say that they'd like tea.

Harry goes on, 'Right, that's the drinks sorted, and I'm very pleased about that.'

'Yes,' says Debbie, 'that is a weight off our shoulders.'

'Things are going very well indeed,' says Eric.

'OK,' says Harry. 'Right, next up, what about snacks? I got Dairylea Dunkers, Wotsits, Fridge Raiders, butterscotch waffles, or would you like me to ask me mam to just bring over a nice selection of biscuits to go with the tea?'

Eric and Debbie quickly agree on just having the biscuits,

so Harry phones his mam up to bring over the tea and the biscuits. Debbie says, 'Ask your mam to bring some serviettes – I don't want to get crumbs on this nice floor.'

Eric butts in, 'Yeah, ask if she can bring some Handy Andies as well – I've got a bit of a runny nose.'

After Harry has done all that, he gets ready to address the gang. He gets all formal, crosses his arms and stands in front of the other two. 'Right,' he says, 'things have got very much out of hand with the Peaky Gooners and it's all become very distressing. Theo was shouting at us directly in our faces during the match on Saturday, which was very upsetting, and after the match, somebody – probably Santi Cazorla – left a tod on the bonnet of Debbie's Fiat 500.

'They have been spreading rumours that Eric has a miniature Johnson, and last week, they came to my mam's house and shouted rude things about my chin into the intercom system, which is not what it's to be used for!'

'That's very hurtful,' says Debbie. 'What did they actually say, Harry?'

Harry says, 'Oh, it was terrible. They said, "Is chinny Kane there? The boot of our car is stuck and we need to use his chin to prise it open." And then they drove off before me dad could catch them and give them a good dressing-down.'

'Oh, that's hurtful,' says Debbie, and he looks like he's going to cry.

'Don't cry, Debbie,' says Harry. 'We have got to toughen up or the Peakys are going to just walk all over us. Now, I think what we are all agreed is that we need to join forces with the Sherwoods. I know Vans and Toby are foreign, but they are that little bit older than us and probably better fighters.'

Debbie butts in: 'In training the other day, Toby kicked a ball so high that it took ages to come back down.'

Eric says, 'Yes, I saw that, Debbie – it went so high that it was a long time before it bounced back on the pitch.'

Harry says, 'So, I think we're all agreed that we need to join forces and incorporate their skill set into an elite unit, like you would get on an exciting film. But I am NOT willing to change our name or club uniform – what say you, Eric and Debbie?'

They other two agree but, just at that moment, there's a screech of brakes outside the garage – it's Toby and Vans. They've got their music up really loud – 'Amadeus Amadeus, Rock Me, Amadeus! Amadeus Amadeus, Rock Me, Amadeus!' – and they're just standing in the doorway of the garage in their green tracksuits, staring and singing.

'Amadeus Amadeus, Rock Me, Amadeus!'

So, Harry, who's not going to be beaten, turns his sound system on and starts singing, 'Let meeeeee... entertaaaaiiin yooouu! Let meeeeee... entertaaaaiiin yooouu!' It's a cultural stand-off.

Harry's mam appears and says, 'Turn that music down!'

'Sorry, Mam!'

'Sorry, Mrs Kane!'

Harry's mam leaves and it's all quiet again. Vans takes a step forward and speaks up. 'Before we go any further, I need to inform you that, if we are to join forces, the name of the gang must be the Sherwoods, and the uniform must be green tracksuits and Robin Hood hats. This is non-negotiable.'

Harry says, 'No way, it's not happening, bro. It will be the White Harts!'

Toby replies, 'Listen, you fool. We are older than you, so we say what will happen.'

Debbie chirps up, 'But, Harry, if we change our name again, that means new business cards, new key rings, new decals for our cars, new necklaces, and that is all very inconvenient.'

'Ditto for us,' says Toby. 'And we also have club tankards, and they would have to be re-enamelled, and that would take up to two weeks, as they would have to be sent off to Innsbruck.

Suddenly, Harry has a bright idea. 'Let me run this past you and see what you think, Vans. What say me and you have a game of table tennis to decide on this difficult issue?'

Toby and Vans put their hands in each other's trouser pockets for a bit and whisper, then Vans turns to Harry and says, 'Game on!'

It's best of five sets, two sets apiece, and it's 20-19 to Harry – match point. Is it going to be the White Harts or is it going to be the Sherwoods? It's a long rally, without either of them giving an inch. Suddenly, Harry's feet give way on some biscuit crumbs that Debbie spilled. He falls on his arm and the bat flies out of his hand.

Debbie's eyes start filling with tears and Eric falls to his knees, thinking this is it: the end of the White Harts. Vans pulls back his forearm, ready to smash the winning shot. Suddenly, Harry leaps up from the floor like a salmon and, using his chin as a bat, fires a winning shot past the despairing Vertonghen.

Harry's chin has won the day and, from this day on, the Spurs gang will forever be known as... the White Harts!

215

THE RETURN OF STEVE'S PRIDE

Steve has been on the up – Casper is back to full fitness, the Fat Lass has slung her hook after he found out she'd been banging Sam Allardyce, and he's signed up for a course to study Sports Management at the Metropolitan University in Manchester.

It's halfway through his first morning on his course and he's already made a new pal – Burnley manager Sean Dyche – and they're having a stand-off between Steve's hair island and Sean's disc beard. They're having a whale of a time together, but it all ends suddenly when Steve's phone lights up on his desk. It's a message... from the Fat Lass.

It reads: 'Hello, Steven. Look who I've got,' and attached is a picture of Casper. He runs straight out of the lecture theatre, shouting, 'Get out of my way! Casper's been kidnapped! Get out of my way!'

He heads straight home and, when he gets there, there's a note written for him on the back of a KFC bucket lid, demanding that Steve meets her at Trafford Retail Park, where the Wickes is. He has to go in the clown car because she's taken the Octavia.

He hammers it down the M62 – 'Honk, honk, honk, honk! Get out of my way, you silly Rodney plonkers – Casper's been kidnapped! HONK, HONK, HONK!' Hair island blowing all over the place.

Steve gets home and sees the Octavia on the drive. He knows the Fat Lass is inside it because the windows are all steamed up with condensation. He pulls open the door and shouts, 'Where is he? Where's my Casper, you nasty bastard?'

'Oh, calm down. Shut up and stop acting the fucking hard man,' she snaps.

'Yes, love.'

He gets in the car – she's eating a large cod and chips with a fishcake, battered sausage, mushy peas, a mince-and-potato pie and a gherkin. She says to him, 'There's a Tracker bar in the glove compartment for you if you want it.'

She goes on, 'Right – this is how it's going to be. Big Sam has moved to the West Indies and I want to go there with him, so I'm going to need two hundred thousand pounds. Don't fuck me about or else Casper's a goner.'

The next day, he's got an interview for the vacant manager's job at Derby County. He turns up at Pride Park in the clown's car, gets out, puts the steering wheel in the boot, winds down the ejector chair, picks the door up off the floor.

There's a doorman there. 'Hello, Mr McClaren. Nice clown's car – could I take your hat and coat for you?'

He says, 'I'm not wearing a hat – that's my HAIR ISLAND! It's my HAAAIIIIRRR IIIIIISLAAAAAND!'

The doorman says, 'It must have got blown about a bit in the car – it looks more like a HAIR HEDGEHOG! A HAAAIIIIRRR HEEEDDGEHHHOOOGG!' to which Steve says, 'Don't be such a Rodney plonker, it's a hair island.'

Steve gets taken to the waiting room outside the board-room, and he sits by the radiator to warm up. It's a bit like Alan Sugar's place in there – a lady at the desk, sofas and that. But he's worried about his hair island ahead of the interview, so he goes to the loo to apply some 'Island Tamer'.

He's got it in a tub and he makes it himself. He uses that waxy residue you get in a ketchup bottle when it's dried up a bit at the top. He gets some of that and he mixes it with the juice from a tin of mackerel. But it's got a bit runny from being next to the radiator and, when he puts it on, it brings all the hair on his island to a point. 'Bloody hell,' he says to himself, 'what a bloody shame.'

While he was sitting in the waiting room, he saw Will Hughes and Chris Martin dressed in white jumpsuits, but that's another story for another time...

Meanwhile, in the boardroom, the chairman, Mel Morris, is interviewing Sean Dyche for the job, and there's a specially commissioned carpet on the boardroom floor, with a huge depiction of the Derby ram mascot on it.

Mel's asking him what he thinks of the stadium, and Dyche says, 'I very much like it. I very much like the design. I very much like the contrast between the black and white seats. I think the stadium very much helps to create a tremendous atmosphere. The only thing I don't like is some of the frou-frou. You know, the pictures of the sheep on the big windows, or this daft sheep carpet on the floor. It gives out very much the wrong message.'

Mel flips his lid at this, and he says, 'I've just had that put in last week! Go on, you can fuck off, trying to tell me how to decorate my office. Go on, fuck yourself, four-four-two style, you ugly twat. You're as bad as Pearson – he was a heathen as well!'

So Dyche leaves the room, all red and puffed up, like a Chinese steam cleaner fully at work, on a deadline and that. As he leaves, he gives Steve that cut-throat motion, as if to say, 'Watch out, it's bad in there.'

Steve goes in next. 'Hello, Mel – nice to see you,' and all that. He's got that swagger that he puts on, like a bit Californian. 'Hello, Steve,' says Mel. 'I see you're sporting a hair javelin,' to which Steve replies, 'No, Mel, it's just my hair island – it's a long story.'

'So, Steve, what do you think about coming back here to Pride Park?' But Steve isn't listening. He's started to shake, and he's having trouble breathing. He falls on to the floor, on his knees, with tears forming in his eyes and his hands rubbing on the carpet.

He says, 'Mel, look at it. It's hand-tufted and knotted with a silk-and-wool blend. I've not seen such quality outside of the presidential suite at the Qatar Bari Bari hotel in Dubai. Oh, look at the sheen on the ram insert! Oh my god, Mel – look at the scrollwork on the ram's horns... FUCK ME, MEL – is the border detail finished in bamboo silk? It can't be! It just can't be!' Then he starts rubbing his hair island against the carpet.

'Yes, Steve,' says Mel. 'It's bamboo silk with one-hundred-per cent hand-twisted yarn. Thank God you're back, Steve. Someone who understands this club; who appreciates that carpeting is more important than football. That's what this club needs – the job's yours if you want it.'

Steve says, 'I do, Mel. Only two conditions. I want a carpet like this in my office and I want to choose my own assistant. How much are you prepared to pay up front for the assistant of my choice, Mel?'

'Two hundred thousand pounds,' says Mel. 'Two hundred thousand pounds.'

With a big smile on his face, Steve says, 'It's a deal, Mel. It's a deal.'

THE ALDERMAN VISITS BOB'S HOUSE

I haven't seen the Alderman for a good few weeks. Obviously, his face and his body shape enters my mind from time to time, and I occasionally go to the website of the *Teesside Evening Gazette* to see if there's any new pictures of him doing his charity work or campaigning on behalf of the dozy kids.

So, I'm at home with the wife last Tuesday; we're having one of our afternoon Crime Clubs, watching a documentary about a bloke who murdered his victims with door handles. As soon as we saw that on the blurb, we booked in the time off to watch it.

You would, wouldn't you? Documentary about a bloke who killed his victims with door handles – you can't imagine anyone saying, 'Naah, I don't want to see that,' so we were watching it.

Anyway, suddenly, there's a very, very robust knock on the door. You think, ooooh, police, bailiff, whatever. It had that sort of authority. It really gave me a bit of a shock, and my cat, who was sat next to me, spewed up all over my Jacamo catalogue as soon as he heard it.

So I went to the door, opened it up... it's the Alderman. He's got his charity minibus parked in my drive and, boy, did he look smart. He was wearing a chocolate-brown wool jacket, and silvery grey slacks that are sort of gently flared at the bottom but still really tight around his thighs and his arse. Really nice, nice contours. Oh, and red shoes.

Obviously, my heart misses a beat and I swallow a bit. 'Hello, Robert,' he says. 'Long time no see.' ('Long time no kiss,' I'm thinking.) 'Well, are you not going to invite me in?'

I said, 'No, no, of course. Lovely to see you. We're just watching a programme about Jake Litchey, the door-handle killer.'

'Oh,' says the Alderman. 'The door-handle killer. It's a very nice choice.'

So we get into the front room – the wife's turned off the telly because she's a bit embarrassed about having it on during the day. I do the introductions and the wife asks the Alderman if she can get him anything to eat. He says, 'Yes, Margaret – thank you. I've got a long journey back to Stockton. Could I have a ham sandwich and a piece of fruit, please?'

'Of course,' says the wife, and the Alderman says, 'Hold on, hold on – ummm, what fruit have you got?'

She says, 'Oh, I've got bananas, pears, apples, oranges...' and he says, 'Do you have appricott, Margaret?'

The wife says, 'Eeeeh, no, I don't,' so I volunteer to go and get some from Waitrose, but he insists that I stay there because he says he needs a chat 'about daft-kids stuff – but I really do need an appricott.'

So Margaret says, 'That's fine, I'll go,' and off she goes to Waitrose.

As soon as she's gone, he says, 'Listen, Robert – as I said, I've got a long journey ahead. Could I have a quick shower?' Which is understandable, so I said of course he could – I showed him where it was and let him get on with it.

A couple of minutes later, from upstairs, I hear, 'Robert! Robert! Can you come and help me, please? Quick, Robert!' So I go upstairs and knock on the bathroom door, and he says, 'Come in, Robert.' I go in and he's stood there, naked in front of the window that overlooks the drive.

He's about seventeen stone, the Alderman, but his skin's still really taut. It's a bit red in a few patches, because my wife always has the shower on too hot, so that's not his fault. Now, because it's late afternoon and he's in front of the window, his shoulder hair is really fluffed up and it's silhouetted in the light coming from the window, like a lovely patch of a camomile lawn or something that you just want to bury your head in.

'I need a towel, Robert. The one you provided fell out of the window.'

So I brushed past his body and I looked down out of the window and, sure enough, there's my towel. But guess who's holding it? The fucking Town Clerk. He's there with all his cronies – the vicar who stinks of bleach, the Head of Parks and Recreations, the whole gang. And Biffy Clyro's even there, drawing on his face.

When they see me, they all start chanting, 'Kiss the Alderman, kiss the Alderman, kiss the Alderman...'

And I'm thinking, 'Yeah, I really want to.' So I turned to him and he's already in position, staring at me with his mouth wide open, as wide as it'll go.

I open my mouth as wide as I can and I slowly, slowly move towards him... and, just as our lips are about to couple, he stops me, puts his hands on my shoulders and his tongue starts darting around my mouth like a little juvenile snake. Then he gently puts my hand against the side of his thigh, and THEN he clamps his lips on to mine.

Both of our lips are quite wet so they're slipping around

each other, sort of searching for a grip. Then he pulls back…
and it's over.

'Thank you, Robert – that will be all.'

Biffy throws the towel up and it comes through the
window, and I quickly go back down to the lounge, but I'm
thinking, 'Wow, what just happened there?'

Anyway, he leaves straight away, before the wife got back
– so I got a kiss AND I got to have the appricotts!

STEVE'S RESTAURANT SHOWDOWN

Steve's got his new job at Derby County, he's cock-in-a-hoop, and he's insisted that the chairman advances him £200,000, which he can use to pay the ransom and get Casper back from the Fat Lass.

He gets outside Pride Park and Sean Dyche, who was interviewed before him, is waiting for a lift back into town to get his bus back to Burnley. Sean's wearing all the ska gear: purple suit, black-and-white check tie, white loafers, leather trilby.

Steve sees him and says, 'Have you been eating a Calippo or pumpkin soup or something, because you've got orange all around your mouth.'

Sean fumes, 'No, no, you awful slag. It's my disc beard. It's my DIIIIISC BEEEAAAAARRD!

'Hey, Steve,' he adds. 'Has a squirrel just burrowed in your head? 'Cos the tip of its tail is still sticking out.'

'Don't be a Rodney plonker – that's my HAAAIIIRRR IIIISLAAAAND! My HAAAIIIRRR IIIISLAAAAND!'

Then they both laugh and Sean asks, 'Can I have a lift to the bus station, Steve?'

'No problemo, Señor Dyche!' because he's one of those who says 'methinks' and 'a pint of your oldest, finest ale, stout yeoman' in pubs because he reckons all that shit's funny.

So they both get in his clown car and Steve's driving

along. HONK, HONK, HONK on the clown-car horn. 'Get out the way, you dipsticks – we've got the Burnley shuttle to catch!'

They start chatting away, and Shaun says, 'Hey, Steve, have you seen Neil Warnock's eyebrows? It's like he asked for a crack wax and the lady thought his face was his arse!' And they laugh.

'Good one,' says Steve. 'Have you noticed that Mark Hughes hasn't got any lips? Looks like he asked for an anal bleaching and the lady thought his face was his arse!' And they laugh again.

'Good one,' says Sean. 'Quite similar to mine, but not bad. You know why he's called Sparky, don't you? 'Cos whenever he plugs something in, sparks fly out of his arse and spell the words EGYPTIAN COTTON.' And they laugh once again.

'Good one, El Maestro,' says Steve. 'Have you seen David Moyes' bulging eyes? It's like he just popped a blackhead on his ball sack... and his face got stuck!' And they laugh yet again.

'Oh. Oh,' says Sean. 'What a lot of fun me and Steve McClaren have had. How do you think you'll get on at Derby?'

'Just the same as before,' says Steve. 'Muddle along, keep smiling until I get the boot and a nice big wad. I call it drift and severance.'

He's dropping Sean off at the bus station, and tells him that he's off to meet the Fat Lass. She'd texted him, saying, 'Meet me at the Maison Valise Ajourd'hui,' which is a really posh place, and it translates as 'The House of Yesterday's Briefcase'.

Sean says, 'Oh, The House of Yesterday's Briefcase – that's a right fancy drum. You'll need a tie,' and gives Steve his black-and-white checked tie to wear, which is nice of him.

Steve heads over to the Maison Valise Ajourd'hui and, when he gets there, he can see that one of the windows in the restaurant is all steamed up, so he knows the Fat Lass must be sat in there near the window. He's got the image of Sam Allardyce pumping away at her on the kitchen table with her legs banging against the baking trays and the biscuit tins in his head, making him shudder. But he pulls himself together and he goes inside, where the maître d' greets him.

''Ello, sir, welcome to the 'Ouse of Yesterday's Briefcase. Can I just say that the mouse on your head is an absolutely adorable thing.'

'No, that's not a mouse on my head,' says Steve. 'It's my hair island. My HAAAIIIRRR IIIISLAAAAND!' Then he goes in and sits down at the table with the Fat Lass, who is obviously ready to go on a trip. She's got suitcases, a ski bag – she's off to Austria. 'Hello, love – you off skiing, then?' says Steve.

'Aww, fuck off, you watery twat. Listen, I'm in a rush so I've ordered the four-bird roast with a side plate of pork chops for me, and a bowl of custard off the kids' menu for you… is that OK?'

Steve replies, 'Yes, of course, love, yes, love, of course, love. Listen – how's Casper? I miss him so much.'

'You'll find out when you pay me my two hundred thousand pounds!'

'Yes, I know, love, I know,' says Steve. 'The money should

be in my account by the end of the meal. Just tell me how he is and where he is. He really needs to be warm…'

'I'm telling you NOTHING until I get me money! Now keep checking your phone and eat your custard.'

So Steve starts to eat his custard, and then he sees the queerest of things. The ski bag behind the Fat Lass seems to be pulsing and moving slightly. There's something inside it and Steve sees it push its head through the flap at the top. Could it be Casper?

It IS Casper, and he manages to poke himself about a foot out of the bag and his throat begins to swell up – he's getting ready to spew. Steve just wants to rush up and hug him, but he knows that it would be too dangerous with the Fat Lass there – she'd kick his fucking face in.

He throws Casper a look to tell him 'Don't you dare – don't do it, Casper', and the swelling in the snake's throat starts to go down. Steve can hardly contain his excitement, but he needs to be able to get to Casper without getting kicked in by the Fat Lass. He's got two options. Create a distraction or disable her.

Then he remembers the time when Casper danced on the black-and-white tiles on the kitchen floor and the contrast of the yellow of the snake on the tiles triggered a fit. He also realises that he's got Sean Dyche's black-and-white tie around his neck.

Thinking quickly, he lets some of his yellow custard drip down on to the tie, then a little bit more, until the Fat Lass notices. 'Fuck's SAKE,' she hisses, and Steve asks her to clean it off for him. She yanks him across the table by his tie and starts rubbing at the yellow stain.

As she's rubbing and rubbing, her eyes start to bog up, and she begins to sweat – it smells like when you've just opened a tin of corned beef. Steve winks at Casper, and Casper winks back at him.

The Fat Lass's fit has now kicked in – she starts shaking, dribbling from her mouth, and her legs start banging on the table legs. Steve jumps up, grabs the ski bag with Casper in it and runs out to his clown car, bursting with happiness.

He's got a new job at Derby, Casper's back in his arms and he can still hear the faint banging of the Fat Lass's legs as she throws a fit in the House of Yesterday's Briefcase.

BOB'S SCOTTISH DIRGES

THE SCOTTISH BAKER

Och, I'm a Scottish baker, I bake the Scottish pies;
I've got problems with my drainage, and problems with my
wife.
The two may be interconnected, 'cos I bludgeoned her to
death
By repeatedly hitting her head with my welder's mask.
I disposed of her flesh and bones, down the back kitchen
sink;
Now my toilet's blocked, and my pie meat's starting to stink.
That will be 40p, Mr McKay, and I would eat it before sunset
If it was my pie.

THE TALE OF MICHAEL MOWBRAY

This is the tale of Michael Mowbray, a man born on a bed of
scouring pooder
And behidden of a heart of, a heart of pure stone.
On his eighteenth birthday, he announced a barn dance;
The price of admission included a free artisan hamburger...
and an amusing badge.
The whole island came, apart from Harry McKay,
Who had a trumpet stuck up his arse from efforts to blow
out an unruly tod.

An unruly tod. An unruly tod.

On the count of midnight, Michael Mowbray called for
   silence;

'Hey, ya bastards,' he growled, 'you know those artisan
   hamburgers?'

'Aye, we do, Michael.'

'Well… they were nae artisan… but frozen ones from Aldi
   on the mainland!'

The more fragile in the audience dropped to their knees in
   pain,

Whilst those of a firmer bollock twisted their faces in temper.

But Michael just smiled as he left the barn,

And tossed a flaming truncheon into its belly.

Eighty lives were lost; eighty lives were lost;

EIGHTY LIVES WERE LOST.

And now only Michael and Mr McKay reside on that
   godforsaken island.

And what about Mr McKay's difficult tod?

And what about Mr McKay's difficult tod?

It fell out exactly one year to the night of the barn dance,

And is now kept in a box with various other 'difficult items';

With various other 'difficult items'.

And that's the end of the tale of Michael.

THE TALE OF SAM MCGREGOR

This is the tale of Sam McGregor,

The last surviving adult male on the island.

He had long harboured dreams of escaping to the mainland,

Where he could sample the pastry at Greggs,

Or visit Costa Coffee, where you could 'apply within'.

Even enrol at a Bannatyne or Pure Living gym, and cleanse his body with their luxury soaps.

He had planned his escape for some time, but things had now turned urgent

As, in the last month... eighty men had died.

EIGHTY MEN HAD DIED.

YES, EIGHTY MEN HAD DIED.

He fashioned a durable craft from discarded fencing;

Oars were made from that little access panel you find on lamp posts,

Which he prised off with a large hinge from his mother's blanket box.

It was past midnight when he dropped his boat into the water

And climbed down the quayside ladder.

Just as he placed his boot into the boat, he heard the water roll and lap,

And there, by the side of the boat, was a large fish, swimming upon its back.

As the moonlight adjusted his eye, he saw that the fish had the face of Brian McDermott.

THE FACE OF BRIAN McDERMOTT.

THE FACE OF BRIAN McDERMOTT.

'What do you want of me, horrible fish? Just let me pass on my way to the mainland.'

'There's no escape from the island withoot consequence – just look at the fucking state of me.

'You must return to your mother right away, boy,' said the fish.

'If you're not back by her side within an hour, then she will
    suffer a fate far worse than that which has been imposed
    upon me and my shoal.'
Sam stared at the surface of the water, and everywhere he
    looked were fish
With THE FACE OF BRIAN McDERMOTT.
THE FACE OF BRIAN McDERMOTT.
THE FACE OF BRIAN McDERMOTT.
Sam climbed up the ladder and ran at all his speed across
    the barren moors;
Just over the hour had elapsed when he entered his mother's
    bedroom.
She appeared to be sound asleep – he placed his hand on
    her shoulder to check for warmth,
When, suddenly, she turned and stared at him fully.
The fish was no' fibbin' – her fate was worse than theirs;
She had the face of Louis van Gaal.
THE FACE OF LOUIS VAN GAAL.
THE FACE OF LOUIS VAN GAAL.
And that's the end of the tale of Sam.

THE TALE OF STEWART MCDERMOTT

This is the tale of Stewart McDermott;
A tall, wiry boy of little conversation, but plenty thought.
Not lonely, but always on his own;
Not depressed, but reflective and gentle in his manner.
Like most of the younger men on the island,
He dreamed every day of leaving to start life on the
    mainland.

There was only him and three other males surviving on the
 mull
For, in the previous nine months,
THIRTEEN MEN HAD DIED.
THIRTEEN MEN HAD DIED.
When he imagined life on the mainland, he saw himself
 striding into Timpson's heel bar
And demanding that his shoes be reshod on one of their
 complicated revolving machines.
Or whistling at the lasses as they gathered around the
 bollards,
Preventing vehicles from entering the housing estate.
He even saw himself sat in Costa Coffee,
Drinking hot chocolate and being handed the wifi code by
 the lassie with tits to spare.
Now, for several years, Stewart had been researching the
 geology of the small island,
And enquiring of the older generation about the infamous
 'Hellpot Hole'.
It was reputed to be the home of an unusual beast,
With whom a deal could be struck to escape the clutches of
 the godforsaken isle.
His research had led him to a small inlet, confusingly absent
 from all maps and records,
And fenced off with barbed wire, on which locals had hung
 various charms and warning bells.
But his desire to leave was strong and so he tunnelled under
 the barrier,
Using the exhaust pipe from a Lambretta scooter that had
 dropped out of a plane

And landed on the moors, killing a man on impact.

As he clambered down the hinny to the entrance of the
Hellpot Hole,

He felt a fear and foreboding usually reserved for those who
dared to stroke a bull's balls with a fistful of nettles.

Entering the cave, he was immediately struck by the stench
of boiled onions

And, sure enough, he soon saw a figure bent over a large
cooking pot,

Stirring onions in a rolling boil of water.

The figure was naked but covered in hair – a branch snapped
beneath his feet,

And the figure slowly turned its head toward him.

Stewart made to run, but his feet were now stuck by a sticky
substance that was leaking from the base of the onion pot.

The beast was now fully turned, and Stewart whimpered,

As he saw that it had the face... of Benny Hill.

THE FACE OF BENNY HILL.

THE FACE OF BENNY HILL.

'Do you like boiled onions?' said the beast. 'I fucking do;

'In fact, I cannae get enough of the wee sweet bastards!'

The beast plucked an onion out of the pot, and held it,
unscalded, in his hand.

He approached Stewart with the onion, held affront of him.

'I sense you want to leave the island, boy?'

'Aye! I do!' said Stewart.

'You'll be wanting to visit Timpson's to have a key cut on
their complicated machine, and other such mainland
nonsense, I guess.'

'Aye! That's right!' said Stewart.

'Well take a bite of the onion, child.

'I will assure your passage through Hellpot and on to a series
    of chambers to the mainland;

'But there is a price to be paid…'

'I'll pay that price,' said Stewart,

And he grabbed the onion and bit into it.

As he chewed, the beast held up a gilded mirror for Stewart
    to gaze upon,

And what he saw brought about his instant demise, simply
    from the shock of it.

He had the face… of Luis Suárez.

THE FACE OF LUIS SUÁREZ.

THE FACE OF LUIS SUÁREZ.

And that's the end of the tale of Stewart.

THE TALE OF MURRAY STIRLING

This is the tale of Murray Stirling;

His eighteenth birthday was fast approaching,

And he knew he must escape the clutches of the island

Before that date, or be forced to spend the rest of his adult life

In the caves 'neath the island,

Digging for precious stones to adorn the laird's new
    ceremonial capes,

And his bongos.

His dream was to start a new life on the mainland;

Many times he imagined himself wearing the orange-and-
    blue tabard of the B&Q Organisation,

Guiding customers toward the wallpaper paste or replace-
    ment fence panelling,

Laughing with colleagues in the staff room as they chatted
to each other

Through short lengths of drain pipe.

Sometimes he saw himself in Café Nero,

Buying a guest bean cappuccino, and requesting an extra
shot

From the waitress with plenty of tit.

And, for sure, he would submit the relevant forms to gain
resident's rights

At Oak Furniture Land, with that portly man and his dozy
son,

And enjoy the cosy lifestyle that it offers.

But, for now, he needed a boat, and that was an illegality on
the island.

The laird employed a giant of a man, known only as 'The
Boatman'.

He would search the island every day for evidence of boat
building,

And would smash what he found with his spiked iron ball
and chain.

The boatman's face was always covered with a hessian
hood,

But it was said that, underneath, he had the face of thirteen
chickens.

THE FACE OF THIRTEEN CHICKENS.

THE FACE OF THIRTEEN CHICKENS.

But Murray was clever – he had assembled his craft inside
the old lighthouse,

A place that no other, including the boatman, would
trespass;

For it was reputed to be the home of Mainland Mary,

A spectre that would devour you with pure buttery love.

Murray knew that such talk was bullwater, so had used the lighthouse as a safe haven to build his boat.

The night arrived, and Murray entered the lighthouse and began to untether his hand-built boat,

Which he had fashioned from hardened turkey tods, joined together with sticky glue.

Suddenly, the room was filled with a golden light,

And his heart was instantly filled with joy.

A figure appeared in front of him, more beautiful than the very centre of desire.

She wore a blue-and-orange tabard, and was seated in an oak dining chair.

Beside her was an occasional table – again, made of oak.

And a bookshelf, made from imported oak.

She had tits to spare and a bottom that stretched her full length.

She slowly leaned forward to offer him a cappuccino,

Ready poured in a paper cup with a wifi code written upon it.

'Drink me, Murray, Murray; drink me.

'Drink me, Murray, Murray; drink me,' she chanted.

She was the mainland and he wanted to reside within her.

Then... BOOM!

The door to the room burst open, and in strode the boatman.

The vision of the lassie dissipated, and he was all alone and in fear.

'She gave you a windae into your life on the mainland,

'But that is all you will ever know of it!'

The boatman began to remove his hessian mask, and what
    Murray saw killed him in an instant.
The boatman had the face... of sixteen owls.
THE FACE OF SIXTEEN OWLS.
THE FACE OF SIXTEEN OWLS.
And that's the end of the tale of Murray.

THE TALE OF MARY MCDOUGALL

This is the tale of Mary McDougall.
Mary was the youngest daughter of Thomas McDougall,
A farmer held in high regard on the island,
As its sole producer of turnips and sugar beets.
Mary had inherited from her father an arse as wide as a
    sheep is long,
But had plenty tit upstairs to compensate for any imbalance.
Her skin was ruddy and well tempered, due to a weekly
    soak in a tub of turnip water,
Heated to lukewarm but no further.
It was the week of her eighteenth birthday;
The date on which she must become the bride of the island
    laird.
Her duty to serve him, both in toil and passion;
Her fate to never leave the laird's castle and bathe in sweet
    turnip water again.
It was Mary's duty to forego her freedom or suffer the pain
    of forced labour
In the caves 'neath the island.
All other lasses had forborne the same fate, but Mary was
    no ordinary lass.

Mary dreamed of escaping to the mainland,

To the bustling artisan coffee shops, with bearded proprietors.

Housing estates with no through roads,

Where a traveller's only option was to make a three-point turn if sucked into its grip.

Wifi hotspots available for free on the registration of a few simple details.

She saw herself rushing to the twenty-four-hour copy shop in Stranraer,

To obtain a large photocopy of her favourite dog,

To hang on the wall of her new accommodation.

When asked what size she required, the laddie would blush,

As she asked for a big one;

Though it would be clear from his awkward stance that he was possessed of

A long and stout personal pipe.

There was only one plan that could see her dreams fulfilled,

And that was to murder the laird.

But the laird was guarded twenty-four hours a day by Petmir;

A beast, part wolfhound, part pig, and part generic animal.

But, worst of all, reputed to have… the face of Olly Murs.

THE FACE OF OLLY MURS.

THE FACE OF OLLY MURS.

But, in this respect, Mary had immunity,

For she, unlike most of her race, had no fear of Murs.

In fact, she was rather warm to the idea of taking the weight off his knacker-pack.

Her plan was simple: on the night of their betrothal, she would hide a dagger in her girdle,

And plunge it into his heart as he clambered upon her.

If need be, she could dispose of the beast Petmir by the same design.

The night arrived, and the laird clambered around her endless behind

To position himself aside her.

She could hear the rhythmic breath of Petmir beneath the bed,

And she knew that she must be swift and certain in her attack.

The laird spoke:

'I am about to rise up and clamber upon you.

'Should you refuse or impart any negative sign towards the act,

'You will be fed to the beast. Do you understand?'

'Aye, I do,' whispered Mary.

The laird made a sudden move towards her girdle,

And Mary found herself frozen as his hand chanced upon the dagger.

He lifted it to the light and pronounced her fate.

'This one is for you, Petmir; show her no mercy!'

Mary turned her head to address her fate,

And what she saw killed her from shock in an instant.

The beast did no' have the face of Olly Murs.

No, it was far more dastardly.

It had the face… of Honey G.

THE FACE OF HONEY G.

THE FACE OF HONEY G.

And that's the end of the tale of Mary.

THE TALE OF CALLUM MCBRIDE

It was Christmas Eve on the island, and young Callum
  McBride was full of wonder and hope,

For the following day would be the biggest day of his
  young life.

His parents, on the other hand, were in a spirit of trepidation
  and fear,

For, you see, the laird had chosen their boy to be the
  centrepiece of his entertainment

At his Christmas feast.

And, for that reason alone, they had decided to effect their
  son's escape to the mainland that very eve.

If they failed, their precious son would be fetched at dawn
  by the laird's henchmen

And taken to await his fate in the castle.

Young Callum's mind was racing.

He had often dreamed of life on the mainland;

The wonder of the Timpson's heel bar, with its revolving
  machine

And its intricate leather-working tools.

Not to mention its sweet-smelling, powerful glues,

Which could work their magic on even the most absorbent
  of materials.

He saw himself wearing a tight blue suit,

Two sizes too small for him, as was the fashion on the mainland,

And striding into Costa Coffee to demand their latest guest
  bean cappuccino.

The waitress would be fulsome of tit and would seat him at
  a table,

Where he could admire her curvature at leisure.

Many times, he had imagined himself dining at the latest pop-up restaurant,

A fusion of Turkish and Rastafarian peasant food,

Served on plasterboard, with drill bits as cutlery.

Occasionally, he dared to imagine himself out on a date at Frankie & Benny's

With the waitress from the coffee shop.

At the bus stop, following their burger meal,

She would turn to him and say,

'Would you agree, young laddie, that I have plenty tit to spare?'

'Aye,' he would reply.

'There's many a helping there, with leftovers for the poor of the parish.'

She would laugh and allow him a brief tap on the side of her bounty.

Fast forward to midnight;

Callum and his parents cower on the beach as a small craft with a single lamp approaches.

'Get in, lad. We must make great haste,' says the man in the boat.

And he does get in, and his parents weep as they say goodbye,

Knowing that the laird would guillotine them for this offence.

Three hours later, Callum stepped off the boat, on to the shore.

'See that light there?' said the boatman.

'That's my daughter. Go to her and she will provide you safe harbour.

'Go on – away you go.'

Callum approached the light, and could nae believe what he saw 'neath its glow.

It was the girl from the coffee shop,

Exactly as he had imagined her.

He smiled an anxious smile as she put down her lamp and began to unbutton her blouse.

When fully undone, Callum was faced with a sight that killed him instantly,

For her tits were not of the expected nature.

They had embedded in them… the faces of Andy Gray and Richard Keys.

THE FACES OF GRAY AND KEYS.

THE FACES OF GRAY AND KEYS.

Back on the shoreline, the boatman pulled back his hood and let out a cracker of a laugh.

It was the laird.

'Merry Christmas, Callum,' he whispered.

And both he and the waitress disappeared in a puff of black smoke.

The next day, Callum's parents received news that their son had passed away on an island beach.

For, you see, he had never left, and now he never would.

And that's the end of the tale of Callum.

A HISTORY
OF FOOTBALL

PART SIX

THE MODERN GAME

May 2011: FIFA overlord Sepp Blatter shocks football fans everywhere by stating that Manchester United do not actually exist, explaining away their glorious history as 'a trick of the light'. Blatter, speaking in Esperanto for some reason, says, 'I can prove that they don't exist and that everything they have supposedly achieved is as a result of mass hysteria. This sort of thing has happened before. It's in the Bible, near the back.' He goes on to describe Alex Ferguson's so-called reign at the club as '… like the story of The Emperor's New Clothes. The whole thing is nothing but a wrinkly old man dancing around in the nude, and contributing nothing.' Blatter adds that he plans to have the club 'excluded from everything ever, with no comebacks' and for Old Trafford to be filled with boiling hot gravel.

As shocked journalists leave the conference hall, the FIFA warhorse mumbles another announcement, declaring that he plans to rebrand football after the 2014 World Cup, renaming it 'Blatterball' and taking a personal 65 per cent cut from all gate proceeds.

July 2011: The Lee Mitchell hostage crisis ends at Brighton and Hove Albion after forty-three days, and the player is allowed to complete his move to Crewe Alexandra. Brighton's caretaker manager, Neil Wallace, had kidnapped the striker after his contract ended and held him in the away dugout, which he sealed up with mud and twigs. When reminded that, under the Bosman rule, Mitchell was free to move, the Brighton boss yelled, 'Send Bosman round here, then – I'll ram his ruling right up his hoop.' Mitchell finally escapes while Wallace is chewing a particularly tricky piece of a Curly Wurly.

January 2012: A match-fixing scheme is uncovered in Italy involving one of Serie A's top referees. Gianluigi Biscotto has been taking cash bribes from players and club officials for fifteen years and is banned for life. Suspicions of his wealth arose when Biscotto started refereeing games while hovering 10ft above the pitch in a solid-gold helicopter, scoffing quail eggs and guzzling rare champagne made from liquidised elephant ivory.

July 2012: Bristol Rovers striker Lee Newman is sent home from pre-season training after reporting back five stone under his usual weight. Newman, who in his spare time is a keen actor, spent the summer break starring in a one-man play about the life of *Carry On* star Charles Hawtrey. When he reports back to the club, officials lock him in a cupboard and force-feed him a special weight-gaining diet of custard pizzas topped with lard, along with a fresh-cream-and-curry shake. Newman suffers a massive heart attack five hours later and is forced to retire from the game.

August 2012: Thirteen teams are expelled from the Fogarty Tools South Yorkshire and District League following new ground safety regulations implemented by the league's controversial chairman, Frank Hampton. Hampton decrees that any club whose automatic hand dryers do not match his own personal specifications will be instantly relegated. He says, 'Some of the contraptions I've come across have had less power than Wayne Sleep farting through his dancing tights. I, and tens of others, don't follow grass-roots football in order to dry our hands on our hard-earned trousers.

These charlatans will have to learn, and I'm teaching them the Frank Hampton way.' The outspoken chairman's own business, Hampton's Hand Dryers, were also recently behind a hostile and, ultimately, unsuccessful attempt to take over the sponsorship of the league.

September 2012: Beleaguered Birmingham manager Lee Clark narrowly avoids an FA disciplinary charge after issuing his first team with mobile phones and texting them instructions during their recent 1-0 cup defeat at Fulham. Clark, who regards himself as a progressive manager, claims he has done nothing wrong, saying, 'I was standing in my technical area the whole time. If sending text messages isn't technical, then I don't know what is.'

But midfielder Darren Ambrose complained, 'There must have been a problem with the T-Mobile reception in the ground. There was nothing for about twenty minutes then we all got a load of texts at once. I was catching up on mine, which included "Kick it harder" and "Go over there", when Steve Sidwell nipped in and scored the winner.'

July 2013: The Premier League proudly announces that this season's match ball will be the first to think for itself. The Umbro Hal 2013 has a high-speed processor chip implanted within a water-resistant black polyurethane foam core, and each ball emits a small noise when it has been filled to optimum level. Furthermore, the Hal 2013 can respond to an individual player's kick. 'Our balls know each player in the Premier League by name,' reveals Umbro spokesman Rick

Danger. 'And the ball will talk to them at regular intervals, encouraging fair play.'

Danger goes on to disclose that the Premier League has also implanted every player's boots with a unique microchip. 'This ensures that, when the time comes, all players can be summoned by a magic signal to our headquarters, in preparation for the overthrow of the government. We at Umbro will no longer be ignored. We are the power, the strength and the way. One day – one day soon – this country will be ours.'

August 2013: Wigan Athletic striker Liam Bell wins his court appeal, which allows him to be able to play with his own ball during matches in addition to and separate from the actual match ball, after claiming that his human rights were being breached. The FA react by launching a similar appeal to Brussels, claiming that their own human rights allow one of their representatives to run on to the pitch and 'put a fucking bread knife through Bell's fucking ball.'

February 2014: Sepp Blatter wakes up from a nap and announces the launch of a fifty-six-team global Zombie League. 'Everyone loves zombie films,' he tells a packed press conference. 'Also, money.'

August 2014: Troubled Cowdenbeath hope to revive their fortunes after signing a player who, they say, is from the future. Manager Jimmy Nicholl says, 'He claims he can teleport his way around the pitch at hyper light speed, but he hasn't actually done it yet, as he picked up a slight thigh strain on his way here. He's also really good at complicated maths, and wears sunglasses like Kevin Spacey's character in *K-Pax*. That's good enough for me and I hope it'll be good enough for our fans.'

The future traveller, who goes by the name of Zeemod 21 and occasionally squeaks when he talks, added, 'This is but a stop on my journey. I will sign for Arsenal in four months. It is destiny. They cannot impede it.'

December 2014: Instead of the traditional players' Christmas party, Chelsea stars choose to take part in a torchlit parade down the King's Road from Sloane Square. With his bare teeth, José Mourinho pulls a float that features a papier-mâché representation of his personal response to Richard Dawkins' book, *The God Delusion*.

Says Mourhino, 'In my art, Dawkins will receive his punishment from God. It will show the heretic Dawkins having his intestines pulled out through his anus by a choir of angels, with God looking on.'

September 2016: Bookmakers suspend betting after jobless legend Ryan Giggs comes from nowhere to become the 5/2 favourite for the job as Temporary Seasonal Sales Assistant at Popcornsville DVD-rental store in Salford. Giggs says, 'Obviously, I'm flattered to be linked with the job, but I won't return to work unless it's the right move for me. I can't say any more at this point.'

Previous frontrunner Lee Baines hits out, saying, 'I've got retail experience from my summer job at Halfords and I'm in the second year of a Film Studies degree. I can see why Popcornsville would look to someone with the calibre of Giggs, but it would be nice if someone would take on a so-called novice like myself once in a while.'

OCTOBER 2016: Concerned at the increasing deluge of top talent being lured to the burgeoning Chinese Premier League and its many riches, UEFA begin slyly injecting players with a special serum that will induce sickness if they step on Chinese soil.

The drug has been developed in UEFA's top secret Swiss laboratory and officials tell players that it actually contains concentrated liquid Haribo, the popular energy source enjoyed by many players before matches.

Wayne Rooney falls foul of the serum when he goes on a 'weekend break' to China a few weeks later, and is confined to his Beijing hotel with severe stomach cramps. Ironically, it later turns out that the pains were caused by an actual overdose of Haribo.

FEBRUARY 2017: Recently-sacked Claudio Ranieri

summons the press to a pool hall on the outskirts of Leicester and announces that his entire spell as manager of the Foxes was 'fake news'. The Italian says that the whole Premier League Champions thing was 'in the minds of the evil mainstream media' and that they can't prove it ever happened.

Ranieri says that he has been a pool hall hustler for the last three years and couldn't possibly have found the time to guide a football team to the pinnacle of the English game.

As assorted members of the media look on, he proves his point by almost potting the eight ball while elaborately holding his cue behind his back, shouting 'Dilly ding, dilly dong!' as he does so.

APRIL 2017: Zlatan Ibrahimovič reveals that his days as a footballer are numbered, and that retirement is imminent. Speaking via a video of a hologram of himself that he successfully uploads to Facebook on the third attempt, the Swedish legend says, 'One day soon, the Zlatan project will be over and you will all be sorry that you said those things. Zlatan will return to his natural form – a spear made from pure crystal – and Zlatan will fire himself directly into the heart of the sun, causing it to shatter into a zillion pieces and bringing an end to life as you know it. Then you will all be sorry that you said those things.'

SEPTEMBER 2017: Middlesbrough owner Steve Gibson finally sells the club after twenty-three years at the helm. The new owner is an anonymous, enigmatic figure who insists on being known only as 'Mr A'. All official club statements are made via his representative, a small, thin man who has a twitch and stinks of bleach. Changes are afoot as soon as Mr A takes charge, with the team wearing a new skin-tight kit and replacing the traditional pre-match opposition handshake with a nice long kiss.

EPILOGUE

FOOTBALL 2050: WHAT THE FUCK?

What will football be like in the future? We've tried to look forward by another forty-five years, or whatever, to the year 2050... here's what our imaginary crystal ball said the beautiful game will be like then, or whatever...

MANAGERS: They simply won't exist any more. Fans will decide team selections, tactics and substitutions and mid-match instructions, using a method of psychic voting where democracy will rule the day!

PLAYERS: Your team's legendary players will never retire, as human cloning will be as normal as getting the dry skin on your feet nibbled by a tank full of fish used to be a few years ago. There'll need to be a limit on how many players from the past can be cloned, though, in order to bring through the youngsters of 2050, or whatever.

CAPTAINS: The role of the team's skipper will continue to grow as the decades roll by and, by 2050, captains will probably spend more time carrying out day-to-day administrative duties. As such, they'll definitely have whatever the 2050 equivalent of a desk is, positioned in the arc on the edge of the penalty area, replete with coffee machine, water cooler and secretarial services. Team-mates will be able to consult with them on a strict appointment basis as the match is played, probably.

HOOLIGANS: Hooliganism is still said to be the scourge of the game, but would it really be so bad if specially selected groups of supporters indulged in some good old-fashioned hand-to-hand combat during the half-time break? A bit like cage fighting, yes? No weapons, just quick wits and even quicker fists. As an incentive, the winning fans' team gets a goal. Would that be so terrible or would it be really, really, REALLY great? Hmmm...

CROSSBAR TENTACLES: Yes, believe it or not, the crossbar as we know it simply won't exist. The 2050 crossbar will be a sentient life form and will have tentacles. When a goalkeeper is getting a bit too warm, he'll be able to instruct his crossbar to waft its tentacles and cool him down. Sounds crazy, but it'll definitely happen, probably!

GIANT GOALS: Fuck it, why not? Humans are growing all the time and, by the time 2050 comes around, goalkeepers will probably all be the same size as Robert Wadlow (ask your dad!). Therefore, it makes sense to increase the size of the goals, and bigger goals equals more goals and more excitement. Goalmouths will definitely become as high as rugby posts and twice as wide as they are now, probably! This will inevitably lead to basketball-type scorelines, and our new giant goalkeepers will be kept on their toes as well. Hey, maybe they could do with a little bit of help...

EXPANDING GOALKEEPERS: Yes, fuck it, why not? By 2050, genetically creating a man/pufferfish goalkeeping hybrid that will be able to inflate himself and fill the entire goalmouth in a split second will be as normal as setting up a direct debit is these days. Although this would probably definitely make it harder for teams to score, even though we've vastly increased the size of the goals, so we're going to need...

EIGHT GOALS: Life will be very different in 2050 and

we'll all have the attention span of a fucking pufferfish, so let's take the two goals at each end of the pitch that we know and love and add a few more in for good measure. Sod it – let's have one extra goal in each of the four corners and two more on the touchline level with the halfway line. Like in snooker, but more. Fuck knows: maybe we'll change the name of football to 'Snooker But More'. Anything is possible, probably. In fact, football can learn so much from snooker – it's a simple sport that works perfectly, so let's also borrow...

KICKING CUES: Fuck, yeah! Modified snooker cues attached to the boots of the players, which they have to use in order to kick the ball, will become the order of the day in 2050. The boots will be attached together on runners to help replicate the cueing action that has made snooker such a global hit. Unfortunately, this is going to make it hard for players to run, so we'll need...

HOVER BOOTS: Scientists promised us stuff like this by the year 2001, but it never happened, so they can't be too far away now – it'll probably definitely happen by 2050. Instead of running everywhere (which, when you really think about it, is a fucking stupid idea), players will float around just above the surface of the pitch, trying to bang the ball past scary fish-men into one of eight massive goals using stupid fucking sticks on the ends of their boots.

TOP HATS TO BE REINTRODUCED: And in snooker too, while we're about it.

KESTRELS FOR REFS: Not sure how this would work – we'll try and come back to you one day.